Exploring Economics

Answer Key

Exploring Economics Answer Key

ISBN 978-1-60999-097-8

Front Cover: Blue jeans by Alexander Mazurkevich / Shutterstock.com
Back Cover: Background by springtime78 / Shutterstock.com

Cover design by Mary Evelyn McCurdy
Interior design by Charlene Notgrass
Content by Ray Notgrass, Charlene Notgrass, and Bethany Poore

Printed in the United States of America

Notgrass History
1-800-211-8793
www.notgrass.com

Unit 1

Lesson 1

1. How did Alfred Marshall define economics in *Principles of Economics*? *A study of mankind in the ordinary business of life (3)*
2. What is the meaning of the Greek word *oikonomos* from which we get the word *economics*? *steward (5)*
3. In previous generations, the word *economy* primarily referred to the management of what? *A household (6)*
4. Today the words economize and economical usually refer to what? *being wise or frugal—that is, being a good manager—in financial matters (6)*
5. List three jobs that economists do. *Students are to list three of these: teach in universities, work for investment companies, write books, give speeches, hold positions in government that enable them to influence economic activity. (6)*
6. How does *Merriam-Webster's Eleventh Collegiate Dictionary* define economics? *A social science concerned chiefly with description and analysis of the production, distribution, and consumption of goods and services. (7)*
7. Production involves the supply of what? *Goods and services available in a society. (7)*
8. Getting goods and services to the public is called what? *Distribution (7)*
9. Individuals, households, businesses, and governments purchasing and using goods and services is called what? *Consumption (7)*
10. What would you like to learn from your study of economics? *Answers will vary.*

Lesson 2

1. An economy in which some authority (usually the government) dictates what and how much producers will produce is what type of economy? *Command (9)*
2. Would you prefer living in a free economy or a command economy? Explain your answer. *Answers will vary.*
3. A society moves toward economic interdependence when workers do what? *Specialize in certain kinds of work that they perform for others for which they receive payment of some kind. (11)*
4. When people realize that they are better off concentrating on certain skills and depending on others for other goods and services, they begin to experience the principle of what? *Comparative advantage (12)*
5. List five things you use frequently for which you rely on the specialized labor of other people and do not know how to create or prepare yourself. *Answers will vary.*
6. The simplest circle-flow diagram includes what two entities? *Households and businesses (12)*
7. On what principle does a market operate? *Supply and demand (14)*
8. The exchange of goods or services in which people determine equivalent values is called what? *Bartering (15)*
9. How is price important to suppliers? *Prices determine whether an individual or a company can survive in the marketplace by supplying goods or services at a certain price and then obtaining other goods and services from other suppliers at certain prices. (15)*
10. Because money enables a person to obtain goods and services that he or she wants or needs, it is a medium of what? *Exchange (16)*

Lesson 3

1. Why do many American companies choose to have their products made overseas? *Cheaper labor (17)*
2. Give four examples of how a country at war can negatively affect trade? *Workers may have to leave their work to go fight in the army; they might be wounded or killed; destruction of factories and farmland; disruption of business within the country and of trade with other countries. (17)*
3. A group of workers who organize themselves and negotiate with business owners for higher wages and benefits is called what? *Labor union (18)*
4. Why do high taxes on income discourage efforts by individuals to generate more income? *Much of what they earn has to go to the government. (18)*
5. How might regulation increase the cost of goods? *Companies pass on the costs of regulation to consumers in the form of higher prices. (18)*
6. What are three examples of institutions that help an economy operate? *Corporations, labor unions, banks (20)*
7. What term describes economic effects external to the direct production of goods? *Externalities (19)*
8. What is the meaning of the term gross domestic product (GDP)? *A measure of the value of all of the finished goods and services produced within a country. (21)*
9. Define poverty rate. *The percentage of the population that lives below what the government determines to be the minimum income to provide needed goods and services (21)*

10. What is microeconomics? *Microeconomics looks at how individual households and companies make decisions and how buyers and sellers interact in the market. (21)*

Lesson 4

1. Who is often called the father of modern economics? *Adam Smith (23)*
2. What book by Adam Smith was published in 1776? The Wealth of Nations (*or* An Inquiry into the Nature and Causes of the Wealth of Nations) (23)
3. The prevailing economic philosophy when Adam Smith published *The Wealth of Nations* was what? *Mercantilism (24)*
4. How did Smith challenge the prevailing view of how nations build and acquire wealth? *He said that the economy actually developed from the bottom up rather than from the top down. (24)*
5. What do those who advocate *laissez faire* economics want government to do? *To refrain from any regulation of economic activity (25)*
6. Where was Karl Marx born? *Prussia (25)*
7. What book did Karl Marx write with Friedrich Engels? The Communist Manifesto (27)
8. Marx divided society into what two classes? *The working class (the proletariat) and the ownership class (the bourgeoisie) (27)*
9. What question is the basic divide between capitalism and socialism? *Who should make economic decisions? (29)*
10. Contrast how Adam Smith and Karl Marx believed economic decisions should be made. *Smith believed they should be spread as widely as possible throughout the economy, while Marx believed that a select few should make them. (29)*

Lesson 5

1. What is seen as the starting point of the influence of the Austrian School of Economics? *The 1871 publication of* Principles of Economics *by Carl Menger (31)*
2. Ludwig von Mises believed a command economic system would be unworkable because of the absence of what? *Free-market competition (31-32)*
3. What events vindicated Ludwig von Mises' belief that the absence of competition in a free market would make a socialist system unworkable? *The downfall of the Soviet Union and Eastern European Communism (32)*
4. *The Road to Serfdom* by Friedrich Hayek influenced what two world leaders? *U.S. President Ronald Reagan and British Prime Minister Margaret Thatcher (32)*
5. Who is considered the father of the modern study of macroeconomics? *John Maynard Keynes (32)*
6. In *The General Theory of Employment, Interest, and Money*, what kind of government action did John Maynard Keynes advocate to stimulate demand in times of emergency? *Deficit spending and the funding of public works (32)*
7. The conference at Bretton Woods, New Hampshire, led to the creation of what three organizations? *World Bank, the International Monetary Fund, and the General Agreement on Tariffs and Trade (33)*
8. In his 1981 inaugural address, what did Ronald Reagan say about government? *That it is not the solution, but the problem (33)*
9. What term describes a key idea of Milton Friedman which highlights the role of money in the economy? *Monetarism (35)*
10. Milton Friedman believed that the Great Depression was primarily caused by what? *A failure of the Federal Reserve System to maintain an adequate supply of money to help the economy grow (35)*

Unit 1 Quiz

1. *c (5)*
2. *c (19)*
3. *d (21)*
4. *b (21)*
5. *b (16)*
6. *b (9)*
7. *a (24)*
8. *c (27)*
9. *d (33)*
10. *b (33)*

Unit 2

Lesson 6

1. According to Deuteronomy 8:7-9, God was bringing the Israelites to a land in which they would eat food how? *Without scarcity (39)*
2. A basic principle of economics is that people have to make choices about what? *Scarce or limited resources (39)*
3. Describe the resources of the place where God placed Adam. *It was a well-watered garden which produced everything of a material nature that Adam needed. (39)*
4. In Psalm 37, what does the psalmist say about the righteous and their descendants? *He has not seen the righteous forsaken or their descendants begging bread. (40)*

5. The conditions in Egypt during the famine mentioned in Genesis 42 and 43 illustrate what economic principle? *Supply and demand (41)*
6. According to Deuteronomy 8:18, how do people get the power to make wealth? *God gives it to them. (41)*
7. What were the Israelites commanded to do with their fields every seven years? *Let them rest. (42)*
8. What were the Israelites forbidden to do when they loaned money to their fellow Israelites? *Charge interest (43)*
9. God promised to bless the land of the Israelites if they would do what? *Listen and obey (44)*
10. List three things that Leviticus 19 taught the Israelites to do as they conducted business and economics. *Leave gleanings in the fields for the poor; use accurate weights and measures; and pay hired men at the end of the day (43)*

Lesson 7

In 1 Samuel 8:10-18 the Lord warned the Israelites about what a king would do. Summarize what the king would do to the Israelites:

1. Sons — *Make them part of the army (45)*
2. Daughters — *Make them perfumers, cooks, and bakers (45)*
3. Best fields, vineyards, and olive groves — *Give them to the king's servants (45)*
4. Male and female servants — *Make them work for him. (45)*
5. Flocks — *Take one tenth of them (45)*
6. In addition to wisdom, what did the Lord give Solomon? *Riches and honor (46)*
7. Who told Solomon that his wisdom and prosperity exceeded the reports she had heard about him? *Queen of Sheba (46)*
8. Who made the government even more economically oppressive for the people of Israel than his father had? *Solomon's son Rehoboam (46)*
9. What generous gifts from God did the Northern Kingdom of Israel use for the false god Baal? *Grain, new wine, oil, silver, and gold (46)*
10. What word picture is used to describe how Judah and Israel lived in safety all the days of Solomon? *Every man under his vine and his fig tree (47)*

Lesson 8

1. What is the most important attitude to have concerning financial matters? *Humility (49)*
2. According to Proverbs 22:2, what common bond do the rich and poor have? *The Lord is the maker of them all. (49)*
3. What three things are mentioned in Proverbs 22:4 as being the reward of humility and the fear of the Lord? *Riches, honor, and life (49)*
4. According to Proverbs 12:11, what will happen to the one who tills his land and what does the person who lacks sense do? *The one who tills his land will have plenty of bread; the one who lacks sense pursues worthless things. (49)*
5. According to Proverbs 24:27, what should someone do before he builds his house? *Prepare his work outside and make his fields ready (50)*
6. According to Proverbs 6:10-11, what is the result of too much sleep and rest? *Poverty and need (50)*
7. According to Proverbs 13:18, what will come to him who neglects discipline? *Poverty and shame (50)*
8. According to Proverbs 13:18, what happens to the person who regards reproof? *He will be honored. (50)*
9. According to Proverbs 10:2, what does not profit? *Ill-gotten gain (50)*
10. Before he saw their destruction, how did the Psalmist react to the prosperity of the wicked? *He was envious. (51)*

Lesson 9

1. According to Proverbs 11:1, how does God feel about a false balance and a just weight? *A false balance is an abomination to the Lord; a just weight is His delight. (53)*
2. According to Proverbs 17:23, what perverts the ways of justice? *A bribe (53)*
3. What does Proverbs 22:7 say the borrower becomes? *The lender's slave (53)*
4. What is the modern term used for becoming surety for the debt of another? *Co-signing a loan (54)*
5. In Proverbs 6, the writer tells his son not even to do what before he delivers himself from being surety for his neighbor? *Sleep or slumber (54)*
6. According to Proverbs 29:7, what does the wicked not understand? *Concern for the poor (54)*
7. According to Proverbs 19:17, what will be the reward for the man who is gracious to a poor man? *The Lord will repay him for his good deed. (54)*
8. According to Proverbs 15:16, what is better than great treasure and turmoil with it? *Little with the fear of the Lord (54)*
9. Proverbs 22:1 says that we should desire what more than great wealth? *A good name (54)*

10. Quote what the writer of Proverbs 30:7-9 asked of the Lord so that the writer would not be full and deny Him, or be in want and steal, and profane the name of God? *Keep deception and lies far from me; give me neither poverty nor riches; feed me with the food that is my portion. (55)*

Lesson 10

1. What group did Jesus describe as "lovers of money"? *Pharisees (57)*
2. The scribes and Pharisees encouraged people to make contributions to the temple instead of doing what? *Using their money to take care of their parents (57)*
3. Other than the kingdom of God, what subject did Jesus address the most in His teaching? *Money (57)*
4. What two masters did Jesus say you could not serve? *God and wealth (58)*
5. What two things did Jesus say would choke the word in a person's life? *The worry of the world and the deceitfulness of wealth (58)*
6. What did Jesus tell people to do instead of worrying about food and clothing? *Seek first God's kingdom and righteousness. (58)*
7. Quote what Jesus said about people's responsibility to government and to God? *"Render to Caesar the things that are Caesar's; and to God the things that are God's." (58)*
8. What was the sin of the rich fool? *He had stored up treasure for himself but had not been rich toward God. (60)*
9. In Luke 4:18, Jesus said He came to preach the gospel to whom? *The poor (61)*
10. Jesus warned about a man gaining the whole world and forfeiting what? *His soul (62)*

Unit 2 Quiz

1. *d (39)*
2. *i (41)*
3. *a (46)*
4. *g (47)*
5. *b (49)*
6. *j (50)*
7. *f (50)*
8. *c (55)*
9. *h (58)*
10. *e (58)*

Unit 3

Lesson 11

1. According to Acts 4:32-35, how did the first believers in Jerusalem see their possessions? *Not one of them claimed that anything belonging to him was his own, but all things were common property to them. (65)*
2. What happened to the money the early Christians brought to the apostles from the sale of their homes and land? *It was distributed to each as any had need. (65)*
3. List the three ways that the early church's economic practices were different from Communism. *The government did not carry out the distribution; the early church did not take over the operation of farms and shops that Christians owned; and the sharing of resources was not compulsory. (65)*
4. Describe what the apostle Paul said in Philippians 4:11-13 about contentment. *He learned to be content in whatever circumstances he was in—with humble means and prosperity; being filled and going hungry; having abundance and suffering need. (66)*
5. What promise did Paul share with the Philippians in Philippians 4:19? *"God will supply all your needs according to His riches in glory in Christ Jesus." (66)*
6. What did Paul tell slaves and masters about how they should treat one another? *Slaves should serve their masters as though they were serving the Lord; masters should treat their slaves with justice and kindness, remembering that they too had a Master in heaven. (66)*
7. What did Paul do to keep from being a burden to the Thessalonians? *Kept working night and day (67)*
8. What command and exhortation in the Lord Jesus Christ did Paul give to people leading an undisciplined life, not working and acting like busybodies? *Work in quiet fashion and eat their own bread. (67)*
9. Summarize James 4:13-17. *Answers will vary, but may include these ideas: We can make plans about what business we plan to do in the future, but we don't know what our lives will be like tomorrow. We ought to say, "If the Lord wills, we live and do this or that." (68)*
10. What does 2 Corinthians 8:9 teach about what the Lord Jesus Christ did for us? *He was rich but became poor for our sakes, so that through His poverty we might become rich. (68)*

Lesson 12

1. Do you agree with Tertullian's statement that "Nothing that is God's is obtainable by money"? Explain your answer. *Answers will vary. (69)*
2. Why did some early believers decide to become hermits? *To escape the influence and defilement of the world (70)*
3. What is the meaning of the Greek word *monos*? *One or alone (70)*
4. The communities where people who wanted to escape the influence and defilement of the world gathered were called what? *Monasteries (70)*
5. After Christianity became legal in the Roman Empire, how did many in the church begin to see the monastics? *As possessing a higher level of spirituality compared to others in the Roman Catholic Church (70)*
6. During the Middle Ages, what was the richest institution in Europe? *The Roman Catholic Church (71)*
7. On the whole, how did Puritans see money? *They saw it as a good thing because it is part of God's creation and they saw it as a gift from God. (71)*
8. Name a former monk who led a movement that rejected traditional Roman Catholic teachings and practices, including the idea that poverty was especially meritorious in God's eyes? *Martin Luther (71)*
9. Why did Puritans on the whole see money as a good thing? *Because it was a part of God's creation (71)*
10. What three Puritan priorities led to economic success? *Hard work, a simple lifestyle, moderation (72)*

Lesson 13

1. The focus on social and economic causes in the name of Christ came to be called what? *Social gospel (73)*
2. Give three examples of Christian causes for social reform that occurred during the last quarter of the nineteenth century and the first quarter of the twentieth century? *Prohibition, better working conditions, and a graduated income tax (73)*
3. Give two examples of Christian causes that wealthy businessmen helped fund. *YMCA, Moody Bible Institute (73)*
4. What was the occupation of Max Weber, the German who published *The Protestant Ethic and the Spirit of Capitalism*? *Economist and sociologist (73)*
5. How did Max Weber define capitalism? *Peaceful, voluntary, and mutually beneficial exchanges (74)*
6. List four aspects of Protestant thought that Weber believed influenced the development of capitalism. *The idea of seeing one's vocation in life as a calling; the belief that discipline and hard work were legitimate ways to honor God and to fulfill one's calling; the rejection of personal luxury; and the worth of the individual (74)*
7. What theology supports liberating the poor from their poverty by opposing those seen as oppressing the poor? *Liberation theology (74)*
8. What place does the lesson mention as the main location where liberation theology developed? *Latin America (74)*
9. Why were people who expected political revolution in Jesus' own day disappointed? *Jesus did not come to bring about a political revolution. (75)*
10. What two terms are used to describe the school of thought promoted by R. J. Rushdoony? *Theonomy or reconstructionism (or Christian reconstructionism) (76)*

Lesson 14

The lesson raised these nine questions. Please answer with your opinions.

1. What standard of living should be a Christian's goal? *Answers will vary.*
2. How should a Christian be engaged with the world in terms of economics? *Answers will vary.*
3. What principles should a Christian businessperson follow in his business? *Answers will vary.*
4. How should a Christian businessperson use his or her profit? *Answers will vary.*
5. Is a Christian guaranteed financial success? Explain your answer. *Answers will vary.*
6. What standards characterize a just economy? *Answers will vary.*
7. Explain whether you want to see a smaller, more efficient, and less intrusive government, or a larger, more activist government? *Answers will vary.*
8. Should wealth be redistributed? Why or why not? *Answers will vary.*
9. What is your view of corporate executives who have large pay and benefits packages? *Answers will vary.*
10. List the three things Micah 6:8 says that God wants from us. *To do justice, to love kindness, to walk humbly with our God. (80)*

Lesson 15

1. What modern day example of greed begins this lesson? *A Walmart employee was trampled when shoppers broke down the front door on the morning after Thanksgiving. (82)*
2. How does Merriam-Webster define greed? *A selfish and excessive desire for more of something than is needed. (82)*
3. What does the prophet Amos condemn in Amos 8:4-6? *Those who trampled the needy, those who were eager for the religious festival to be over so that they could trade dishonestly again, and those who were willing to treat the poor as things in order to have more themselves (82)*
4. How did John the Baptist say that people should feel about their wages? *Content (82)*
5. What did Jesus teach the man who was being greedy about an inheritance? *To be on his guard against every form of greed, for not even when one has an abundance does his life consist of his possessions (82)*
6. What does Paul say greed amounts to? *Idolatry (83)*
7. How did greed manifest itself during the building of the transcontinental railroad in the 1860s? *The men who oversaw companies received huge fortunes; workers were paid relatively little and sometimes late. (83)*
8. Greed was a factor in what historic event in America in 1929? *The stock market crash (84)*
9. According to 1 Timothy 6:6-10, what happens to those who want to get rich? *They fall into temptation and a snare and many foolish and harmful desires which plunge men into ruin and destruction. (86)*
10. What does 1 Timothy 6:9-10 say is the root of all evil? *The love of money (86)*

Unit 3 Quiz

1.	*d (65)*	6.	*e (74)*
2.	*h (65)*	7.	*i (73)*
3.	*a (70)*	8.	*f (80)*
4.	*b (71)*	9.	*g (83)*
5.	*j (74)*	10.	*c (82)*

Questions on *Silas Marner*

1. In two or three paragraphs, examine how the author develops the character of Silas Marner through the story. How does Marner change, and what are the causes? *Answers will vary, but may include: At the beginning of the book, Silas Marner is strong in faith in God and in other people. He seems innocent and vulnerable. When his best friend betrays him, Silas Marner offers little defense, but permanently leaves his community. He is angry at the injustice he has suffered. He moves to a distant, remote village, lives alone, and only interacts with people as necessary for his trade. Silas Marner becomes obsessed with the gold that he earns. It becomes the thing that he lives for. His fear, isolation, and distrust only increase as he hoards his money. He is shattered when his money is stolen. The arrival of a toddler, Eppie, completely changes Silas' life. As he cares for her, his world is opened to the power of giving and receiving love. He devotes his life to her well-being, and through her, returns to his faith in God and to healthy connections with other people. His relationship with her leads to peace and wholeness for him.*
2. Refer to Freytag's Pyramid shown on p ##. Write down what you think is the element, event, or section of Silas Marner that correlates with each element of the pyramid: *exposition; narrative hook; inciting incident; rising action; climax; falling action; resolution; denouement.* Answers will vary, but may include:

Exposition: the description of Marner's life with his religious community, his betrayal, and his settling in Raveloe

Narrative hook: the conflict between Dunstan and Godfrey, the revelation of Godfrey's secret marriage and child

Inciting incident: Dunstan steals Silas' money and disappears.

Rising action: Silas and the community search for and speculate about the money; the party at the Cass home

Climax: Molly dies and Eppie comes into Silas' life.

Falling action: Eppie's life with Silas, Godfrey's life without her

Resolution: Dunstan's body and Silas' money are discovered

Denouement: Eppie's refusal of Godfrey's offer and her marriage to Aaron

3. Write two or three paragraphs about the mood or tone of Silas Marner. Why do you think the author employs this mood? How does it help make the story effective? Are there any exceptions to the general mood in the narrative? Answers will vary, but may include: *The mood of Silas Marner is generally dark and sad. The story begins with William Dane's unhappy betrayal of Silas. Silas withdraws to Raveloe and withdraws into his work. The descriptions of his apparent epileptic seizures add to his strangeness and distance from people. Meanwhile, the Cass family is dysfunctional: Squire Cass is detached, his sons are in conflict and they both lack character. Dunstan's thievery and disappearance are shrouded in darkness. The townspeople engage in idle speculation and arguments. The New Year's Eve dance at Squire Cass' house should have been a festive occasion, but it was marred by Godfrey's troubling situation. Molly's death and Marner's shocking appearance holding Eppie in his arms upset the entire community.*

   The narrative brightens as Silas rears Eppie. Eppie brings Silas happiness. Dolly Winthrop and her simple faith and kindness bring brightness to the story. Godfrey and Nancy get married, but their marriage has shadows: they are not able to have children, and Godfrey hides the secret of his being Eppie's father. Eppie's statement of devotion to Silas is a victory of love over money. The marriage of Eppie and Aaron ends the story on a bright and hopeful note.

   The point is that money does not buy happiness, neither for the Cass family nor for Silas. Only human love and genuine relationships bring true happiness.

Unit 4

Lesson 16

1. What was the economic purpose of the first Spanish settlements in the New World? *To extract as much wealth from the land as possible and return it to Spain (89)*
2. An economic system in which a government encourages and assists businessmen in establishing colonial outposts is called what? *Mercantilism (89)*
3. Before the American Revolution, the basis of the economy in the American colonies was what? *Agriculture (90)*
4. What was the primary standard of wealth in the English colonies in America? *Land (90)*
5. What action did King George III take in 1763 that frustrated colonists? *He forbade settlements between the Appalachian Mountains and the Mississippi River. (91)*
6. What weakness did the Articles of Confederation have in regard to taxes? *The national government had no power to tax; it could only request payments from the states and the states were free to ignore those requests. (92)*
7. How did the U.S. government issue bonds to fight the American Revolution? *Wealthy individuals loaned money to the United States by buying bonds, with the expectation of getting their money back plus interest. (93)*
8. What is hard money? *Gold or silver (93)*
9. What was the grievance that farmers had that resulted in their rebellion under the leadership of Daniel Shays? *What they felt was unfair treatment by creditors to whom they owed money (93)*
10. What economic difficulty worried people who lived between the Appalachian Mountains and the Mississippi River? *The federal government could not guarantee them access to the port of New Orleans. (93)*

Lesson 17

1. The fiscal powers given to Congress in the Constitution were significant but were also what? *Limited (95)*
2. According to the Constitution, the national government could regulate commerce with what three entities? *With foreign nations, with Indian tribes, and among the states (95)*
3. Why do you think it is important that the national government fix standards of weights and measures? *Answers will vary.*
4. What crime involving money did the Constitution specify that the federal government could punish? *Counterfeiting (96)*
5. What prohibition in the Constitution helped to unify the nation's economy? *A ban on internal tariffs (96)*
6. Name three benefits of the federal government issuing bonds, as Alexander Hamilton suggested. *Provided revenue for government expenditures; demonstrated that the new government would stand by its obligations; gave bond buyers a strong reason to support the new government (95-96)*
7. What was the main source of income for the federal government for many years? *Tariffs (97)*
8. What controversial institution did Congress charter in 1791? *Bank of the United States (97)*

9. List three innovations that spurred economic growth in America in the late 1700s and early 1800s? *Water-powered spinning frame, cotton gin, steamboat (98-99)*
10. What waterway enabled New York City to become the chief financial center of the United States? *Erie Canal (99)*

Lesson 18

1. What French and British practice hurt American trade during the war they fought against one another in the early 1800s? *Intercepting American vessels (101)*
2. What did the Embargo Act of 1807 require of American ships? *They couldn't leave port bound for Britain unless they paid a large bond. (101)*
3. What was the effect of the Embargo Act on American business? *It caused a serious loss of trade. (101)*
4. How did the federal government fund the War of 1812? *By borrowing from state banks (102)*
5. What was rechartered in 1816? *Bank of the United States (102)*
6. What did the federal government sell to help pay off debt after the War of 1812? *Frontier lands ((102)*
7. What international events contributed to the Panic of 1819? *The Napoleonic Wars ended, causing a decline in demand for American agricultural products, and Britain found a cheaper source for cotton in the East Indies. (103)*
8. What effect did the Supreme Court's decision in *Gibbons v. Ogden* (1824) have on the U.S. economy? *Created a national economy based on free trade and guided only by Congress instead of a patchwork of conflicting state regulations (103)*
9. What was Andrew Jackson's response to Congressional renewal of the Bank of the United States in 1832? *He vetoed it. (103)*
10. What was the name of the system begun in 1840 to hold federal funds and pay the federal government's bills? *Independent Treasury or Subtreasury System (105)*

Lesson 19

1. What was the economic impact of the Civil War in the North and in the South? *The northern economy grew and the southern economy was largely destroyed. (106)*
2. The Morrill Land Grant Act enabled public lands to be sold in order to establish what? *State agricultural and mechanical universities (107)*
3. What did the American economy become by the 1890s? *The largest economy in the world (107)*
4. What was the first big business in the U.S., which grew dramatically after the Civil War? *Railroads (107)*
5. What is the type of business that bankers such as J.P. Morgan participated in which built large enterprises that did not make things themselves, but invested huge sums of money in companies that did? *Investment capitalism (107)*
6. What two tentative steps did the federal government take in 1887 and 1890 to guide business along ethical lines? *Interstate Commerce Commission and the Sherman Anti-Trust Act (108)*
7. What type of company precipitated the Panics of 1873 and 1893? *Railroad (109)*
8. A leader in what industry caused the Panic of 1907? *Copper mining (110)*
9. What did Congress establish in 1913 to serve as the central bank for the United States? *Federal Reserve System (110)*
10. How did federal involvement in the economy change as a result of President Franklin Roosevelt's policies during the Great Depression? *The federal government played an active role in trying to recover from the collapse. (110)*

Lesson 20

1. What two sources of credit encouraged consumers to spend more during the 1950s? *Credit cards and home mortgages (112)*
2. What U.S. president encouraged a large tax cut in the early 1960s in order to spur the economy? What was his party? *President John F. Kennedy, Democrat (112)*
3. What programs of the 1960s greatly increased federal spending and deficits? *President Lyndon Johnson's social programs, such as Medicare and Medicaid, and the war in Vietnam (112-113)*
4. What was the major economic problem of the 1970s? *Inflation (113)*
5. What type of economics did President Ronald Reagan propose in 1980? *Supply-side (114)*
6. Describe how the type of economics Reagan proposed is supposed to work. *When government cuts taxes, people work harder and generate more income which in turn increases the amount of taxes available to the government. (114)*
7. What industry had many failures during the late 1980s and early 1990s? *Savings and loan institutions (115)*

8. What made it possible for people to become millionaires quickly in the 1990s? *The dot-com boom in Internet businesses (115)*
9. What was the average annual growth in the gross domestic product of the United States for the fifty years following World War II? *3% (112)*
10. What are the reassuring words of Jesus from Matthew 6:34? *So do not worry about tomorrow; for tomorrow will care for itself. Each day has enough trouble of its own. Matthew 6:34 (116)*

Unit 4 Quiz

1. *f (89)*
2. *j (90)*
3. *a (93)*
4. *c (97)*
5. *d (95)*
6. *n (99)*
7. *i (99)*
8. *m (101)*
9. *e (97)*
10. *k (101)*
11. *g (107)*
12. *b (107)*
13. *p (107)*
14. *l (108)*
15. *h (110)*
16. *o (112)*
17. *t (116)*
18. *r (114)*
19. *q (115)*
20. *s (113)*

Unit 5

Lesson 21

1. List three simple decisions you have made so far today. *Answers will vary.*
2. List three of the most important decisions you have made in your life thus far. *Answers will vary.*
3. List five of the most important decisions you expect to make in the future. *Answers will vary.*
4. Imagine that you have to choose whom you are going to marry today. List three traits you consider to be essential for that person to have. *Answers will vary.*
5. Name one decision you have made in the past that you would change now if you could. *Answers will vary.*
6. Imagine that you have an important decision to make today. Name three people you would trust to give you wise counsel. *Answers will vary.*
7. Name five decisions your parents have to make that you don't have to make yet. *Answers will vary.*
8. What is the best decision you have made in your life thus far? *Answers will vary.*
9. List the consequences you have experienced so far from that decision. *Answers will vary.*
10. The lesson mentioned two historic events in which the results turned out differently from how the decision-makers intended. Name the events and the consequences. *The Treaty of Versailles helped cause World War II. Loans that were too large for people to pay back helped cause the economic recession of 2008. (121)*

Lesson 22

1. What are three basic economic questions that people in a society decide? *What goods and services, and in what quantities, will an economy produce? How will people produce goods and services? How will people distribute the goods and services across the population? (123)*
2. What is involved in a cost-benefit analysis? *Determining the cost and the benefit of taking a particular step before you take it to determine if the benefit outweighs the cost. (125)*
3. Give an example of a cost-benefit analysis by an individual (one not given in the lesson). *Answers will vary.*
4. Give an example of a cost-benefit analysis by a business (one not given in the lesson). *Answers will vary.*
5. Give an example of a cost-benefit analysis by government (one not given in the lesson). *Answers will vary.*
6. In economics, what is a margin? *A small step that makes a big difference in an action being taken (127)*
7. What is a marginal cost-benefit decision? *Determining the point where a change in behavior occurs (127)*
8. What is a marginal benefit? *The change in total benefit that results from an action (127)*
9. What is marginal cost? *The change in total cost that results from an action (127)*
10. What is the marginal propensity to consume? *The fraction or decimal part of extra income that an individual or household is likely to spend instead of save (127)*

Lesson 23

1. Define goods. *Tangible items that companies or individuals produce for consumption (129)*
2. Define services. *Intangible duties that people perform for pay (129)*
3. What are production resources? *The elements that producers use to create goods and services. (129)*
4. What are material resources? *Those things found in nature or processed from things found in nature that people use to manufacture goods. (129)*
5. What do human resources include? *Labor, creativity, and technology (130)*

6. How is the word capital used in terms of economics? *Materials used to produce goods (13)*
7. Define production possibilities curve and draw a production possibilities curve for a society which can make two products: 1,000 pounds of ice cream and 1,000 pounds of cake. *The production possibilities curve is the maximum production that an economy can have, given its production resources. (130)*

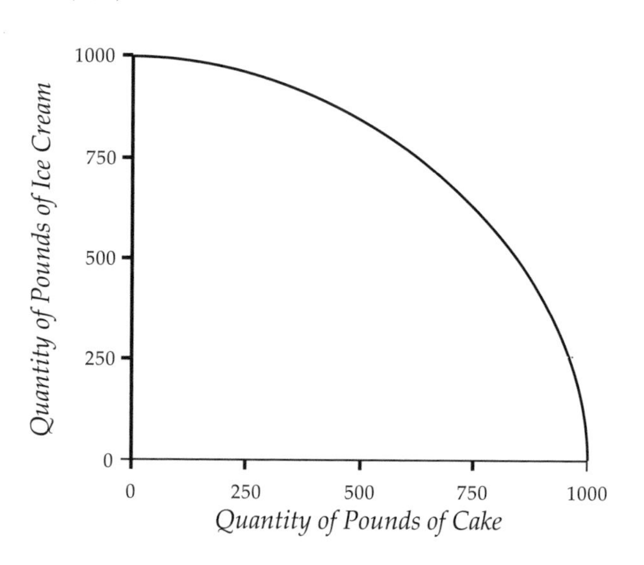

8. Define opportunity cost. *The greatest benefit that a producer gives up when he makes a choice. (131)*
9. When does economy of scale occur? *When the average total cost per item decreases as the number of units produced increases. (132)*
10. When does economy of scope occur? *When a company's average total cost of production decreases as it produces more related products. (133)*

Lesson 24

1. What percentage of economic activity in the U.S. consists of personal consumption? *About 70% (135)*
2. What is an economic incentive? *An economic benefit that motivates action (135)*
3. Name two common incentives for consumers. *Lower prices and subsidies, such as a rebate (135)*
4. Name two disincentives related to cigarettes. *Additional tax and warning labels (136)*
5. What is involved in marginal rate of substitution? *How much of one product a consumer is willing to give up in exchange for another product to maintain the same level of satisfaction (137)*
6. What does consumer choice theory examine? *How consumers decide what to buy (137)*
7. Businesses want to know what four factors involved in consumer choice? *What consumers want, what they can afford, what they choose, and how changes in price and income affect their choices. (137)*
8. How many potato chips in an individual serving bag do you think you could eat before the economic law of diminishing marginal utility would come into play for you? *Answers will vary.*
9. Do you agree or disagree with the idea that a dollar of benefits to the poor will increase their utility (satisfaction) more than a dollar more in taxes will decrease the utility of the wealthy? *Answers will vary.*
10. After reading the section about looking at college from an economic standpoint, what are you currently thinking about your own decision regarding college? *Answers will vary.*

Lesson 25

1. How do capitalism and socialism differ in terms of who makes economic decisions? *In a market economy, the people who participate in the market of buying and selling goods and services make the decisions about who gets what and for what price. In a command economy, government officials make the decisions about who gets what and for what price. (141)*
2. Define economic efficiency. *The goal of encouraging the people in an economy to be as productive as possible in making goods and services available for consumers (141)*
3. Define economic equity. *The goal of having people in a society share goods and services as equally as possible. (142)*
4. What does the principle of economic freedom involve? *Allowing people to do what they want to do in an economy (143)*
5. How does the promise of economic security relate to economic freedom? *The promise of economic security means that you give up a degree of economic freedom. (143)*
6. What is the relationship between growth and stability in both a market economy and a command economy? *Market economies enable growth by risking stability. Command economies try to insure stability while sacrificing the possibility of significant growth.* (143)
7. Name one way the U.S. government provides an incentive for people who own a home. *By allowing homeowners to deduct from their taxable income the interest they pay on a home mortgage loan (144)*

8. What is the basic question a government must answer in relation to the allocation of goods and services? *Will goods and services be available only to those who can afford them, or will they be available to all, regardless of their ability to pay, by means of government funding for them? (144)*
9. Government policies that place limitations on business activity limit the choices that producers and consumers have in order to do what? *Meet other goals that the people in government value (144)*
10. According to public choice theory, what is the basic motivation for voters and elected government officials? *Self-interest (145)*

Unit 5 Quiz

1. *k (121)*
2. *h (125)*
3. *a (127)*
4. *l (127)*
5. *i (129)*
6. *c (129)*
7. *e (130)*
8. *f (131)*
9. *g (135)*
10. *j (137)*
11. *b (129)*
12. *d (130)*
13. *n (136)*
14. *s (141)*
15. *m (145)*
16. *r (141)*
17. *o (142)*
18. *t (143)*
19. *p (144)*
20. *q (143)*

First Exam (Units 1-5)

Matching (2 points each):

1. *c (5)*
2. *g (19)*
3. *n (24)*
4. *j (97)*
5. *o (203)*
6. *p (107)*
7. *f (116)*
8. *m (114)*
9. *i (129)*
10. *r (139)*
11. *a (127)*
12. *e (129)*
13. *b (127)*
14. *d (135)*
15. *l (129)*
16. *h (110)*
17. *k (131)*
18. *q (137)*
19. *t (141)*
20. *s (145)*

True/False (2 points each):

21. *F (9)*
22. *T (16)*
23. *T (21)*
24. *T (143)*
25. *F (143)*
26. *F (29)*
27. *T (136)*
28. *T (130)*
29. *T (130)*
30. *F (89)*

Questions (7 points each):

31. *Microeconomics is the examination of how individual households and companies make decisions and how buyers and sellers interact in the market. (21)*
32. *In a command economy, some authority (usually the government) dictates what and how much producers will produce. (9)*

Fill in the Blanks (2 points per word):

33-34. *supply, demand (41)*
35-36. *God, wealth (58)*
37-38. *kingdom, righteousness (58)*
39. *monasteries (70)*
40-42. *justice, kindness, humbly (80)*
43. *possessions (82)*
44-45. *poverty, riches (55)*

Unit 6

Lesson 26

1. What is a market? *Anywhere sellers offer goods and services and buyers purchase them (150)*
2. Define these terms:
   - capital goods—*Things for which people make a major investment and use to produce other items*
   - producer goods—*Items such as tools and raw materials that people use to make other products*
   - consumer goods—*What end users purchase to meet their wants and needs and what they consume*
   - durable goods—*Goods intended to last a long time (150-151)*
3. Name three indicators of economic freedom. *The kinds and amounts of the goods and services that are available in the market, the ability of consumers to obtain those goods and services in the market, and the ability of producers to bring new and improved goods and services to the market (151)*
4. Why is a market economy sometimes called a consumer economy or consumer-driven economy? *Because the driving force in a market economy is what consumers want and are willing and able to buy (151)*
5. When does imperfect competition take place? *When there is a limited number of suppliers or buyers and one of either can have a significant effect on price (152)*
6. How does competition among "widgets" lead to a better quality of life? *People benefit from owning widgets and more people have jobs producing them. (153)*
7. Define these terms:
   - collusion—*Secret cooperation for a dishonest purpose*
   - cartel—*A group of providers that engage in collusion to increase profits (153)*
8. What is a boycott? *An organized action by buyers to bring attention to what they see as a wrong policy in an attempt to change that policy (153)*
9. Define restraint of trade. *Coercion to enforce a boycott (153)*

10. What do you believe is the fairest economic system for people who are poor? *Answers will vary.*

Lesson 27

1. Define supply. *The total amount of a product or service that is available for purchase (156)*
2. Define determinants of supply. *The factors that a producer considers when deciding what product or service to supply in the market and in what amount to supply it (156)*
3. What is the law of supply? *All else being constant, as the price for a product or service increases, production will increase. (156)*
4. Define demand. *The total amount of a product or service that consumers are willing to purchase at a given price (158)*
5. Define determinants of demand. *The factors involved in causing consumers to purchase goods and services (158)*
6. What is the law of demand? *All else being equal, when the price of a product or service rises, demand falls. (158)*
7. What is the law of supply and demand? *The price of a product or service adjusts to bring supply and demand into balance. (159)*
8. What does Say's Law assert? *That the production, or supply, of products creates a demand for products (161)*
9. Define the macroeconomics term, aggregate supply. *The total quantity of goods and services that all sellers are willing and able to provide at any price. (163)*
10. Define the macroeconomics term, aggregate demand, and list its four components. *The total of all goods and services that all households, companies, and the government are willing and able to buy at any given price in a given period of time. Its components are consumption, investment, government spending, and net exports. (173)*

Lesson 28

1. Define price in economic terms. *What consumers pay when they buy a product or service and what suppliers receive when they sell a product or service (164)*
2. Define cost in economic terms. *The supplier's cost of production (165)*
3. Define price maker. *A producer who has enough influence in the market to have an impact on what price is charged for its product or service (165)*
4. Define price taker. *A producer who has little influence on the market by itself and is forced to charge the prevailing price for its product or service (165)*
5. What does a relative price demonstrate? *The value that one product or service has compared to another (166)*
6. What price factor has contributed to America's great wealth and economic strength? *Businesses have lowered prices for goods and services, which has brought more buyers into the market. (166)*
7. What is price discrimination? *Selling the same product to different consumers at different prices (166)*
8. What is a price ceiling? *A maximum-allowable price set by the government that is below the market-clearing price (168)*
9. What is a price floor? *A minimum-allowable price set by law that is above the market-clearing price (168)*
10. What is another way to express the diamond-water paradox? *Paradox of value (168)*

Lesson 29

1. What causes markets to change constantly? *The goods and services that producers supply and the goods and services that consumers want are constantly changing (171)*
2. When does price stability exist? *When prices in an economy do not change significantly over a long period of time (174)*
3. What is elasticity? *A measure of how much supply or demand changes as a result of changes in other factors (175)*
4. What is price elasticity of demand? *A measure of how much demand changes in response to changes in price (175)*
5. What happens to demand if the price changes for a product or service consumers see as a necessity? *Demand will change little. (175)*
6. What is cross-price elasticity of demand? *A measure of how much demand for one product changes because of a price change for another product (176)*
7. What does income elasticity of demand show? *How much demand changes with regard to consumers' income (176)*
8. What does price elasticity of supply show? *How much the quantity supplied changes because of price (176)*
9. What is the meaning of the term sticky in economics? *Sticky means slow to change. (177)*
10. When does a supply shock occur and when does a demand shock occur? *A supply shock occurs when the amount of goods or services available for sale increases dramatically or when the amount of goods and services decreases dramatically. A demand shock*

occurs when there are dramatic increases in demand for a product or service or when there are dramatic decreases in demand for a product or service. (178)

Lesson 30

1. When does market failure occur? *When the market fails to allocate resources efficiently (179)*
2. What advantage does the seller of a product or service have when that seller has a monopoly? *The seller controls the entire supply of goods or the service in a certain region without other suppliers or customers having a close substitute. (179)*
3. Define these terms and give an example of each:
   - oligopoly—*An oligopoly is where there are only a few large providers, and any one of those providers can have an impact on the market. Example: the passenger jet construction industry. (181)*
   - monopsony—*A monopsony is a market in which there is only one buyer or only one significant buyer. Example: the military aircraft industry or the National Football League. (182)*
   - oligopsony—*An oligopsony is a market in which there are only a few major buyers, any of which can exert a significant influence on the market. Example: large national grocery store chains or tobacco companies (182)*
4. Why does a monopoly cause market failure? *Because a company with a monopoly does not have to set its price as a result of competition (182)*
5. What is the position of a monopolist or of oligopolists sometimes called? *Market power (182)*
6. How can taxes cause market failure? *By increasing the cost of goods and services (182)*
7. Define externalities and give two examples. *Externalities are the effects from supply and demand activity that affect people who are not the actual buyers and sellers in a transaction. Examples of externalities are pollution and smoking. (183)*
8. Define private goods and public goods. *Private goods are goods that one person, household, or company owns and consumes. Public goods are goods and services that more than one person, household, or company can use at a time. (183)*
9. What knowledge did Communist bureaucrats lack? *All of the knowledge diffused throughout millions of producers and consumers that enables markets to work (184)*
10. What do we need to keep in mind regarding markets and an uncertain economy? *All markets will eventually fail, so we should be sure that our most important investment—our very self—is in the hands of the One who will never leave us nor forsake us. (185)*

Unit 6 Quiz

1. *imperfect competition (152)*
2. *oligopsony (182)*
3. *market (150)*
4. *cartel (153)*
5. *supply (156)*
6. *law of supply (156)*
7. *law of demand (158)*
8. *law of supply and demand (159)*
9. *aggregate supply (163)*
10. *aggregate demand (163)*
11. *price (164)*
12. *cost (165)*
13. *relative price (166)*
14. *price floor (168)*
15. *price discrimination (166)*
16. *price elasticity of demand (175)*
17. *cross-price elasticity of demand (176)*
18. *market failure (179)*
19. *public goods (183)*
20. *externalities (183)*

Unit 7

Lesson 31

1. Define money. *Assets that are immediately available for exchange in a transaction, including currency, coins, and deposits in bank accounts (189)*
2. To what does liquidity refer? *The ease with which an asset can be turned into money (189)*
3. What is the significant value of money? *What it represents and what it can do (190)*
4. What does it mean that money is a "medium of exchange"? *It is a commonly agreed-upon object of value to both parties in an exchange. (190)*
5. How is money a representation of value? *It is a way to show value to those with whom you are doing business. (190)*
6. How does money serve as a store of value? *Money gives you a way to store up value so that you can make purchases in the future. (190)*
7. How is money a unit of accounting? *Money is a way to demonstrate success or failure in a business or other endeavor. (191)*
8. What is commodity money? Give the most common example. *Money backed by a commodity that has value in itself. Gold is the most common example. (191)*
9. When is a currency based on the gold standard? *When paper money that a government issues represents gold (191)*
10. What is fiat currency? *Money that has value not based on its relation to a commodity but by a nation's government declaring that its money is legal tender (193)*

Lesson 32

1. How do banks help increase productivity and how do they create wealth? *Banks increase productivity by using people's savings to make loans to businesses so that the businesses can grow. Banks create wealth by enabling the buying and selling of goods and service. (197)*
2. What is the process of banks creating wealth called? *Multiple-deposit expansion (197)*
3. What is fractional reserve banking? *A bank's practice of loaning out the majority of money that it has on deposit. (198)*
4. What is the FDIC and how does it help individual depositors? *Federal Deposit Insurance Corporation. It guarantees that the deposits people have made in a bank will be there (up to a certain maximum dollar amount) and that depositors can withdraw it. (198)*
5. Name four financial products that a retail bank offers. *Savings accounts, checking accounts, money market accounts, and certificates of deposit (198)*
6. What are credit and interest? *Credit is the ability to carry debt. Interest is the price of borrowing money. (198)*
7. Describe the unique function or structure associated with each of these financial institutions:
   Savings and loan or thrift —*Make mortgage loans to home buyers (199)*
   Credit union —*Functions like a bank, but are cooperative ventures that depositors own (199)*
   Mortgage company — *Make mortgage loans to home buyers (199)*
   Investment bank — *Make loans to larger businesses for capital projects (199)*
8. In terms of the money supply of the United States, what do M1 and M2 include? *M1 is the total of currency, traveler's checks, deposits payable upon demand, and other checkable deposits. M2 includes the items of M1 plus money market mutual funds, savings, and small time deposits. (201)*
9. What does the velocity of money tell? *How often the same money is used in transactions during a given period of time. (201)*
10. What is the meaning of credit rating? *A determination of a person's credit worthiness in the eyes of the financial system. (201)*

Lesson 33

1. What is the simplest form of investment? *A loan (203)*
2. What is a bond, what entities usually issue bonds, and what is the issuer of the bond obliged to do? *A bond is a certificate of indebtedness. The issuer of a bond is usually a business or a unit of government. The issuer of the bond is obligated to pay back the face value plus the interest stated in the bond. (203)*
3. What is a purchaser of stock purchasing? *A small part of the ownership of the company that issues the stock. (204)*
4. What is the broad term that encompasses stocks, bonds, and other financial investments? *Securities (205)*
5. What are mutual funds and how do they work? *Investment companies that offer shares to the public. Many individuals invest in a mutual fund, and the fund pools the money so that all investors in the fund share mutually in its growth or decline. (205-206)*
6. What is a money market fund? *Mutual funds that make investments in safe but low-yield investments such as savings bonds or certificates of deposit that have a relatively short time until maturity (207)*
7. What are two popular forms of mutual fund investments that are used for retirement? *IRA (or individual retirement account) and 401K fund (206)*
8. What type of funds take risks by buying and selling securities in anticipation of what fund managers think the securities are going to be worth in the future and are usually available only to wealthy or highly trained investors? *Hedge funds (207)*
9. What does stock or commodity futures trading involve? *Buying stock or commodities (which are often agricultural products) in anticipation of what the future price will be. (207)*
10. What are capital gains taxes? *Taxes on the gain or increase in value of capital assets such as stocks and property (207)*

Lesson 34

1. How do economists define inflation? *A general, across-the-board increase in prices throughout the economy, to the point that it affects almost all people (209)*
2. Define hyperinflation and give an historic example. *A huge and rapid increase in the cost of living, such as what people in Germany experienced in the early 1920s. (210)*
3. What two factors were the main causes of increased government expenditures in the 1960s? *The federal government dramatically expanded social programs such as Medicare, Medicaid, and welfare and it spent huge sums on the war in Vietnam. (211)*

4. How did the federal government pay for those? *The government borrowed money to cover some of the debt, but it also simply printed more money to pay for the increased spending. (211)*
5. What two factors caused stagflation in the early 1970s? *Significant inflation along with rising unemployment (211)*
6. What is deflation? *An overall decline in prices (211)*
7. What causes demand-pull inflation? *An increase in aggregate demand that is not accompanied by an increase in aggregate supply (212)*
8. What is cost-push inflation? *A decrease in aggregate supply which leads to a decrease in productivity, a decrease in supply, and a resulting increase in prices for scarce resources (212)*
9. When does a wage-price spiral occur? *When producers and consumers both try to protect themselves from the effects of expected inflation (213)*
10. What is purchasing power? *The ability of individual consumers to buy goods and services, at least in the short run (213)*

Lesson 35

1. Though the Federal Reserve System is essentially a private bank, what is its relationship to the federal government? *The federal government created it; the president nominates its leaders and the Senate approves them; it submits regular reports to the Speaker of the U.S. House of Representatives. (216-217)*
2. What entity oversees the Federal Reserve System? *A seven-member board of governors whose offices are in Washington, D.C. (217)*
3. What entity oversees the Federal Reserve System's main tool for implementing national monetary policy? *The Federal Open Market Committee (FOMC) (217)*
4. What entities of the Federal Reserve System are located in major cities across the country? *The twelve Federal Reserve regional banks (217)*
5. What banks maintain accounts in the Federal Reserve regional banks and are members of the system? *All federally-chartered banks and some state-chartered banks (217)*
6. What are the four areas of responsibility of the Federal Reserve System? *To implement federal monetary policy; to supervise and regulate the banking industry; to maintain stability in financial markets; and to provide financial services to banks, the United States government, and foreign entities. (219)*
7. What does the Federal Reserve officially issue? *The coins and currency that the United States Treasury Department produces. (219)*
8. Why is the money supply said to be elastic? *The amount of money available in the economy can rise or fall depending on conditions. (219)*
9. What three primary tools does the Federal Reserve System use to manage the money supply and accomplish the nation's economic goals? *1) It can adjust the reserve requirements for how much cash banks must have on hand. 2) It adjusts the discount rate that it charges banks for loans of its funds. 3) It conducts open market operations, in which it buys and sells U.S. Treasury bonds and other federally-issued securities to inject money into or to withdraw money from the economy. (220)*
10. What is the federal funds rate, who sets a target federal funds rate, and how often do they meet? *The federal funds rate is the interest that banks charge each other for overnight loans. The Federal Open Market Committee meets about every six weeks and sets a target federal funds rate. (220-221)*

Unit 7 Quiz

1. *e (190)*
2. *q (191)*
3. *a (193)*
4. *i (198)*
5. *c (199)*
6. *j (200)*
7. *f (203)*
8. *d (203)*
9. *b (204)*
10. *n (205)*
11. *g (205)*
12. *r (207)*
13. *l (207)*
14. *h (207)*
15. *k (209)*
16. *t (213)*
17. *o (217)*
18. *m (219)*
19. *s (220-221)*
20. *p (220)*

Questions on *The Rise of Silas Lapham*

1. What do you think is the theme of *The Rise of Silas Lapham*? (Theme refers to the universal idea that the story conveys.) Write a paragraph explaining your reasons, referring to specific elements of the novel. *Answers will vary. Themes suggested may be similar to the following: Character is more important than status; happiness is not found in material success; love for other people must trump other priorities; one only finds peace when he is true to himself. Student should have written a paragraph explaining evidence for the theme they suggest.*
2. A feeling of pity by one character for another is a thread running through the novel. Identify three instances of this, and explain what happens as a result. *Answers will vary, but may include:*

   Silas Lapham felt pity toward Zerilla and her mother. He helped them with money and advice over many years. He provided Zerilla a job. He kept this a secret from his wife, which was a strain on their relationship.

Mrs. Corey subtly expresses pity toward the Lapham family. She can easily see they are not genteel society. She half-heartedly attempts to accept their friendship.

Mrs. Lapham pities her younger daughter Irene for her broken heart over Tom Corey. She neglects and slights Penelope because she is overwhelmed with pity for Irene. The Laphams take great care to help Irene recover from the disappointment, yet fail to support Penelope.

Tom Corey feels pity for Silas Lapham, though he tries to hide it and maintain a respectful demeanor. He patiently listens to Silas' boasting and bluster. Tom is gracious about Silas' behavior at the dinner party. He tries to help him out of his financial difficulties. Tom is loyal to Silas through his downfall.

3. Write a letter of advice to one of the characters in the story as they face a crucial decision or situation. Write at least two or three paragraphs. *Answers will vary.*

Unit 8

Lesson 36

1. In economics, what does the term trade most often describe? *Purchases between countries. (226)*
2. Define export. *Goods and services that producers create within a country and then sell and send to people, companies, or governments in other countries (226)*
3. Define import. *Goods and services that producers in other countries make and then people, companies, and governments purchase and bring into a different country (226)*
4. How is trade a voluntary exchange? *It involves decisions that people make freely and that no one forces onto someone else. (226)*
5. When does a person practice specialization? *When he or she concentrates on one kind of work and uses the profits from that work to buy the other things he needs (228)*
6. What do people who go against the tide of specialization by trying to be self-sustaining do? *Produce as many goods and services themselves as they can (228)*
7. When does comparative advantage exist? *When one producer has a smaller opportunity cost of producing a good or service compared to another producer (229)*
8. When does absolute advantage exist? *When one person or country can produce goods with a smaller input of resources than another (230)*
9. From your knowledge of climate and geography, explain why Canada has an absolute advantage over Honduras in making maple syrup and Honduras has an absolute advantage over Canada in growing bananas. *Maple trees need a cooler climate and bananas need a warmer one.*
10. What is the difference between comparative advantage and absolute advantage? *Comparative advantage compares what producers give up to produce something, while absolute advantage compares what producers use to produce something. (230)*

Lesson 37

1. What are trade restrictions? *Government policies that hinder, complicate, or eliminate trade between nations (231)*
2. What is purpose of policies of protectionism? *To protect domestic industries from what the government in that country sees as unfair competition from foreign industries (231)*
3. What is an import tariff? *A tax placed on goods that businesses import into a country (231)*
4. Name two purposes of import tariffs. To *raise revenue for a government and to protect domestic industry (231)*
5. Name three negative consequences of American import tariffs. *1) They lead to higher prices for consumers. 2) They lead to decreased consumption which lowers production, which can lead to fewer jobs. 3) It makes other countries less likely to buy the goods and services of American companies. (232-233)*
6. How do import quotas affect the amount of goods that can be brought into a country? *They allow only a certain number to be brought in. (233)*
7. What is a sanction? *An order forbidding citizens from trading with another country (233)*
8. Name one country that has experienced sanctions protesting one of its policies and tell what policy was protested. *Student may answer either South Africa, apartheid (or racial segregation); Iraq, the invasion of Kuwait; or North Korea, development of a nuclear weapons program (234)*
9. What are subsidies? *Government payments to industries that have to compete in a world market where prices are lower than they are in the producing country (237)*
10. Give an example of American products that receive subsidies. *Agricultural products* (237)

Lesson 38

1. Name three results of the Smoot-Hawley Tariff of 1930. *Other countries retaliated with tariffs on American goods, America's foreign trade fell by more than half, and the law cost American jobs and probably contributed to the severity of the Great Depression. (238)*
2. What new pattern of trade did Franklin Roosevelt begin? *Negotiating reciprocal trade agreements with individual nations (238)*
3. GATT and WTO are abbreviations for what? *General Agreement on Tariffs and Trade and World Trade Organization (238)*
4. NAFTA is an abbreviation for what? *North American Free Trade Agreement (238)*
5. NTR is an abbreviation for what term? *Normal Trade Relations (238)*
6. NTR replaced MFN, which means what? *Most Favored Nation (238)*
7. How extensively has the U.S. extended NTR status? *The U.S. has extended NTR status to most nations of the world. (238)*
8. Give four examples of transaction costs. *Import tariffs, fuel expenses, business taxes, and costs of complying with regulations. (240)*
9. What is the purpose of the fair trade movement? *To help families and small companies in less-developed countries compete in the world economy (240)*
10. What are your thoughts about the Milton Friedman quote at the beginning of Lesson 38: "Underlying most arguments against the free market is a lack of belief in freedom itself"? *Answers will vary.*

Lesson 39

1. What are two typical ways that Americans invest in foreign business? *1) American companies invest money to build factories or set up businesses in other countries. 2) Americans buy the stocks or bonds of foreign companies. (243)*
2. As of June 2016, what was the value of U.S. Treasury securities held by foreign investors? *More than $6 trillion (244)*
3. As of June 2016, what two countries held the most U.S. Treasury securities? *Mainland China and Japan (244)*
4. What is a country's balance of trade? *The difference between its imports and exports (245)*
5. When does a country have a trade deficit? *When it imports more than it exports (245)*
6. When does a country have a trade surplus? *When it exports more than it imports (245)*
7. What is the balance of payments? *The record of all transactions between the people of one country and the rest of the world (245)*
8. What is included in the U.S. current account or net foreign assets? *The sum of the U.S. trade balance, the net factor income (interest and dividends Americans receive from foreign investments plus money Americans living in another country send back to their families in this country), and net transfer payments such as direct foreign aid (245)*
9. What has been the main motivation for American businesses "moving production offshore"? *To reduce labor costs (246)*
10. What often happens to individual workers and to communities when an American company moves production offshore? *Workers lose their jobs and communities are hurt. (248)*

Lesson 40

1. What is a currency exchange rate? *The price of one country's currency expressed in terms of another country's currency (251)*
2. How do the forces of supply and demand determine the price for money? *When the supply of a currency in currency exchange markets is greater, its value is less. When demand increases for a currency, its value increases. (251)*
3. What is the equilibrium exchange rate? *The exchange rate at which currency demand equals currency supply (251)*
4. What is the nominal exchange rate? *The rate at which you can exchange one currency for another (252)*
5. In terms of money, how do businesses make purchases of products from other countries? *They use their own currency to buy the currency of the country from which they are buying. (253)*
6. How do higher interest rates set by the Federal Reserve's Federal Open Market Committee affect foreign investment? *They encourage foreign investment in the United States. (253)*
7. What is the real exchange rate? *The rate of exchange for goods and services between one country and another (254)*
8. What is arbitrage? *A term used for taking advantage of price difference (254)*
9. What was China accused of doing some years ago to manipulate the value of its currency to its own advantage? *Pegging the value of the yuan artificially low and then buying huge amounts of American currency (257)*
10. How did this policy encourage other countries to buy Chinese goods? *Those other countries could buy the yuan cheaply to pay for Chinese products. (257)*

Unit 8 Quiz

1. *j (230)*
2. *e (229)*
3. *m (226)*
4. *a (226)*
5. *g (226)*
6. *o (228)*
7. *b (231)*
8. *t (231)*
9. *c (233)*
10. *q (235)*
11. *f (238)*
12. *h (238)*
13. *d (240)*
14. *i (240)*
15. *p (245)*
16. *k (245)*
17. *s (251)*
18. *l (245)*
19. *n (252)*
20. *r (254)*

Unit 9

Lesson 41

1. In the United States, we usually refer to the producers and distributors of goods and services as what? *Businesses, companies, or firms (259)*
2. What is the most common type of business organization in the United States? *Sole proprietorship (260)*
3. Describe how a business partnership is organized. *Two or more people agree to start a business and share in the profit or the loss. (261)*
4. What form of business organization involves a charter, a board of directors, and officers? *A corporation (262)*
5. Describe the difference between a private and a public corporation. *A private corporation is a company that a relatively few people, often just family members, own. This kind of corporation rarely sells its stock to anyone else. A public corporation usually has many shareholders who buy and sell shares of stock in the stock market. (263)*
6. What does LLC stand for? *Limited liability company (261)*
7. What is a PC? *A professional corporation, which physicians, attorneys, or other professionals form to separate their professional liabilities from their personal finances (263)*
8. What is the purpose of a non-profit corporation? *It exists to provide or promote services for the public good. (263)*
9. What is a 501(c)(3)? *A federally-recognized charitable organization (263)*
10. Give examples of three types of non-profit corporations. *Hospitals, charities, and groups that promote the arts (263)*

Lesson 42

1. Define small business. *A small business is privately owned and operated, has under 500 employees, and is not dominant in its field. It can be either a sole proprietorship, a partnership, or a corporation. (265)*
2. What is another term for a very small business? *Microbusiness (265)*
3. If you could own your own small business, what would you like to offer as goods or services? *Answers will vary.*
4. What is a colloquial term for a family-owned business, usually with no more than ten employees? Name a small family-owned business that your family uses. *A "mom and pop operation"; answers will vary. (265)*
5. How many employees are usually employed by a mid-sized small business? *Between 100 and 500 (265)*
6. What percentage of U.S. companies hire less than 500 people? *99.7% (266)*
7. How many new small businesses survive for five years? *About half (267)*
8. What term is often used for an individual who starts a new business? *An entrepreneur (267)*
9. The practice of a local business purchasing the right to use the name and business model of a large company is called what? *Franchising (266)*
10. What was the name and occupation of the woman who became a believer in Jesus in Acts 16? *Lydia, a seller of purple fabric (268)*

Lesson 43

1. Why do you believe many people see selling as a morally questionable activity? *Answers will vary.*
2. If you were going to start a small business, from whom would you seek advice? *Answers will vary.*
3. When someone wants to start a business, they should make an appraisal of what? *Their talents and interests (270)*
4. What is a Unique Selling Proposition or USP? *Something a business can advertise to potential buyers that will help those buyers know how its product is different from and better than products its competitors offer (271)*
5. Who are the best and most important customers a business has? *Those they already have (271)*

6-10. List five key factors that usually determine whether a business will succeed or fail. *6. Management 7. Planning 8. Money 9. Location 10. Overexpansion (Student can list answers 6-10 in any order) (273)*

Lesson 44

1. How does a businessperson determine profit? *By calculating total revenue and subtracting total cost (275)*
2. How is revenue calculated? *The selling price of the goods times the quantity sold (276)*
3. What is accounting profit? *The profit that an accountant determines and that shows up on the books: revenue minus the costs (rent, utilities, price of materials, labor, and so forth), which he can enter into a ledger (276)*
4. How does an economist determine economic profit? *By subtracting the opportunity cost as well as the ledger costs from the revenue (276)*
5. Define fixed costs and give two examples. *Expenses that have to be paid regardless of the rate of production. Rent payments and insurance are examples of fixed costs; other answers possible. (277)*
6. Variable costs are expenses that change depending on what? *The amount of production taking place (277)*
7. What is marginal analysis? *A study of factors that lead to a change in business behavior (277)*
8. What does the law of diminishing marginal returns state? *That the productivity of an input decreases as the quantity of the input increases (278)*
9. What is the production function? *A comparison of the quantity of inputs to the quantity of outputs (279)*
10. What is a deadweight loss? *A reduction in efficiency that leads to a loss in profit or a loss to society (280)*

Lesson 45

1. What are a series of economic expansions and contractions called? *The business cycle (282)*
2. What is the first phase of a business cycle? *Expansion (282)*
3. What characterizes a business expansion? *Increases in the real gross domestic product, growth in the number of jobs, higher average household income, greater business profits, numerous business expansions, and the formation of many new businesses (282)*
4. What is the turning point of a business cycle when the GDP, household income, and profits have reached their highest level and unemployment is at a relatively low level? *A peak (282)*
5. What is the phase of significant decline in real GDP, income, and profits and of rising unemployment? *Recession (283)*
6. What is a trough? *The turning point in the cycle at which economic activity reaches a low ebb and from which an expansion follows (283)*
7. What calendar time does a complete business cycle encompass? *The time between two peaks or two troughs (284)*
8. What term do some economists prefer over business cycle? *Economic fluctuations (284)*
9. How can a natural disaster, such as a hurricane or earthquake, lead to a contraction or slowing down of the economy? *By interrupting supply (284)*
10. What did Milton Friedman believe was the cause of economic fluctuations? *The money supply not keeping pace with output (284)*

Unit 9 Quiz

1. *sole proprietorship (260)*
2. *business partnership (260)*
3. *corporation (262)*
4. *501(c)(3) (263)*
5. *small business (265)*
6. *microbusiness (265)*
7. *entrepreneur (267)*
8. *franchising (266)*
9. *money (273)*
10. *Unique Selling Position (271)*
11. *revenue (276)*
12. *fixed costs (277)*
13. *marginal analysis (277)*
14. *deadweight loss (280)*
15. *economic profit (276)*
16. *business cycle (282)*
17. *trough (283)*
18. *economic fluctuations (284)*
19. *supply (284)*
20. *money supply (284)*

Unit 10

Lesson 46

1. How do people earn income? *By exchanging their work for pay (289)*
2. What is the price of labor? *Wages or salary (29)*
3. What determines the price that buyers (namely, employers) pay for labor? *Supply and demand (290)*
4. Define total labor demand. *The aggregate demand for labor by all firms in an economy (290)*
5. Define total labor supply. *The aggregate of choices that individuals make to enter the labor market (290)*

6. List five reasons that changes in the labor supply occur in a perfectly competitive labor market. *1) Population growth or decline (involving rates of birth and immigration), 2) the age of the work force (the ages that the labor force encompasses), 3) changes in training possibilities, 4) changes in benefits, 5) changes in the nature of the work force (such as more women or minorities becoming part of the labor force) (290)*
7. Give four examples of factors that cause deviations from the labor supply in a perfectly competitive labor market. *1) Wage restrictions (such as a minimum wage law), 2) unions that dictate the price of labor, 3) monopsonies (a single buyer for labor that can dictate wages), and 4) product monopolies (a single supplier that again can set wage rates) (290)*
8. How does the U.S. Department of Labor define the labor force in the United States? *All people sixteen or older who are employed or actively seeking work (291)*
9. List four reasons why a person may decide to become a worker. *Desire for income, wanting personal fulfillment, wanting to serve others, wanting to serve God. (291)*
10. What is the highest purpose of work? *Glorifying God (292)*

Lesson 47

1. For most of the twentieth century, how did economists define white collar positions? *Professional occupations in which people received an annual salary, worked in an office, and had an administrative or oversight role (293)*
2. For most of the twentieth century, what did blue collar jobs involve and how were they paid? *Manual labor, often performed in a factory setting or outdoors; they generally received an hourly wage. (293)*
3. What types of jobs have people described as pink collar and green collar? *Pink collar — Jobs that women have traditionally held; Green collar — Jobs related to producing goods and services that are environmentally friendly (294)*
4. Of the twenty-three Standard Occupational Classifications the federal government has established, which two interest you the most and which two interest you the least? *Answers will vary. (294)*
5. Name two common ways that companies eliminate positions on their payrolls. *Outsourcing and downsizing (295)*
6. Define outsourcing. *Having a private contractor outside the company perform certain tasks (295)*
7. List three changes that may be either causes or effects of a greater percentage of women entering the workforce. *An increase in daycare businesses, fast food restaurants, and processed food products in grocery stores* (296)
8. What does assuming that certain people do not deserve the same pay or the same opportunities introduce into the labor market? *Inequity* (297)
9. When discrimination based on prejudice leads to a misallocation of resources, what is the result? *An economy that dishonors God, dishonors people made in His image, and is less than optimally efficient. (297)*
10. What do artificial limitations such as discrimination prevent in the economy? *They keep it from growing as fully as it could without those limitations. (298)*

Lesson 48

1. Workers organized unions to bargain collectively with industry owners regarding what three issues. *Wages, hours, and working conditions (299)*
2. What does a state's closed shop laws require? *In certain industries, workers have to be members of a labor union. (300)*
3. States that do not require union membership are called what? *Open shop or right to work states (300)*
4. Define featherbedding. *Requiring a certain number of workers for a particular task or location, even if the job did not require that many workers (300)*
5. What type of workers do today's largest and strongest unions represent? *Government workers (301)*
6. List two labor unions which represent government workers. *National Education Association (NEA) and the American Federation of State, County, and Municipal Employees (AFSCME) (301)*
7. Why do economists call unions a cartel? *Because they are organizations that limit the supply of labor in the market (302)*
8. Unions have contributed to a decline in the number of workers hired in what two industries mentioned in the lesson? *Mining, railroading (302)*
9. How have unions impacted union wages and non-union wages? *They have helped to raise union wages and lower non-union wages. (303)*
10. How are unions examples of tradeoffs? *Certain unions have enabled their workers to earn a higher income, but at the price of fewer people working in those industries and crafts. (304)*

Lesson 49

1. What is the difference between a wage and a salary? *A wage is an hourly rate paid for labor rendered; a salary is pay for a job performed regardless of how long it takes to do the work (305)*
2. What are benefits? *Things of value that employers provide which are usually not taxable (305)*
3. Give two examples of benefits. *Employer contributions toward health insurance coverage and contributions to a retirement fund (305)*
4. List three things employers automatically withhold from employee paychecks and send to the government. *Income taxes, Social Security contributions, and Medicare contributions (306)*
5. What is a person's gross income? *The total of his income from wages or salary (306)*
6. What is another term for take-home pay? *Net income (306)*
7. What does functional distribution of income measure? *Income among different businesses and occupations in the economy (306)*
8. What does household distribution of income measure? *The distribution of income among groups of households according to income ranges, regardless of what jobs the people in those households do. (307)*
9. What is the minimum wage? *A legally mandated minimum hourly wage that all employers (with some exceptions) must pay workers. (308)*
10. Considering the pros and cons of a minimum wage, do you think the federal government should require employers to pay a minimum wage or not? *Answers will vary.*

Lesson 50

1. What does the level of employment in an economy indicate? *Productivity (313)*
2. To whom does frictional unemployment refer? *Those who simply have not had the time to find a job. (313)*
3. Why does structural unemployment occur? *Because of a mismatch between the skills that people have and the needs than employers have. (313)*
4. Why does seasonal unemployment occur? *Employers let go employees they hired temporarily during a particular season, and those workers may need time to find other work. (314)*
5. What causes cyclical unemployment? *Downturns in the business cycle (314)*
6. What causes classical unemployment? *Wages being above the equilibrium rate (314)*
7. How is the rate of unemployment calculated? *By dividing the number of people who are without a job but wanting to work by the total work force (314)*
8. What is the generally accepted range of the natural rate of unemployment? *1% to 5% (315)*
9. The term underemployment refers to whom? *People who are working at jobs that are beneath their skill level but that are the only work they can find (315)*
10. What is meant by discouraged workers? *Those who have not been able to find work and have stopped actively looking (315)*

Unit 10 Quiz

1. *g (305)*
2. *n (290)*
3. *a (291)*
4. *s (295)*
5. *c (299)*
6. *k (300)*
7. *d (300)*
8. *q (301)*
9. *h (302)*
10. *e (305)*
11. *l (305)*
12. *f (308)*
13. *i (313)*
14. *o (313)*
15. *b (314)*
16. *t (314)*
17. *r (314)*
18. *j (314)*
19. *m (315)*
20. *p (315)*

Second Exam (Units 6-10)

Terms (3 points each):

1. *g (150)*
2. *d (163)*
3. *a (156)*
4. *j (158)*
5. *b (183)*
6. *q (193)*
7. *c (200)*
8. *m (209)*
9. *e (228)*
10. *h (231)*
11. *f (235)*
12. *i (245)*
13. *k (245)*
14. *p (282)*
15. *r (305)*
16. *o (290)*
17. *l (315)*
18. *n (313)*

Fill-in-the-blank (2 points each):

19. *sole proprietorship (260)*
20. *small business (265)*
21. *entrepreneur (267)*
22. *value (190)*
23. *securities (220)*
24. *fluctuations (284)*
25. *union (300)*
26. *government (301)*
27. *comparative (245)*
28. *trade (238)*
29. *cartel (153)*
30. *supply (156)*
31. *price (164)*
32. *public goods (183)*
33. *credit (199)*
34. *currency (219)*
35. *underemployment (315)*
36. *fixed (277)*
37. *franchising (266)*
38. *exports (226)*
39. *sanction (233)*
40. *deficit (245)*
41. *floor (168)*

Unit 11

Lesson 51

1. What is economic freedom? *Freedom to work, buy, save, and engage in all other economic activity without any hindrance, regulation, or oversight by the government (319)*
2. What do people who believe in economic security think that a country's economic system should provide? *The essentials of life for every member of society whether or not they can afford to pay for those essentials themselves (319)*
3. How does Congress participate in fiscal policy? *Enacting laws related to taxing, spending, and regulations (320)*
4. How does the executive branch participate in fiscal policy? *Through the executing of laws, through regulatory activities, and through implementing policy goals (321-322)*
5. What is the responsibility of the Congressional Budget Office? *Providing "independent analyses of budgetary and economic issues to support the Congressional budget process" (321)*
6. What is the Council of Economic Advisors? *A three-member group of economists that advises the president on domestic and international economic policy (322)*
7. What is the responsibility of the United States Trade Representative? *Developing trade and conducting trade negotiations with other countries (322)*
8. What does the Office of Management and Budget do? *Heads the development of the federal budget and sees that the executive departments follow through on budget guidelines (322)*
9. What Cabinet department is most involved in federal economic policy? *Treasury (322)*
10. What is the purpose of the Internal Revenue Service? *To enforce the tax code (322)*

Lesson 52

1. Name the four purposes of the fiscal and monetary policies of the federal government. *To promote economic growth and stabilization (that is, seeking to avoid significant upswings and downturns), to reduce inflation and unemployment, to encourage international trade, and to preserve the fairness of the free market, as well as equal access to the free market. (325)*
2. When market failure occurs, what is a rare response that involves bureaucrats? *Nationalizing an industry (326)*
3. What kind of environmental policy might a government enact when a market failure occurs? *Taxing or charging fines to polluters, requiring companies to clean up toxic waste dumps, requiring companies to pay the expenses for reducing their level of pollution (326)*
4. What did the federal government do when corn-based ethanol did not prove to be an economically feasible energy alternative to petroleum? *The government began paying subsidies to farmers and producers for its production. (326)*
5. What are the two reasons that the free market does not provide some goods and services? *1) Private companies cannot make a profit doing so; 2) it would be inefficient or unreliable for a private company to do so. (326)*
6. What two security services do most people believe that government should provide? *National defense and local law enforcement (327)*
7. What role do government and private contractors play in building roads and bridges? *Government funds them with tax revenue; private contractors usually do the construction work. (327)*
8. What are the limits to the Temporary Assistance for Needy Families program? *The program has a five-year limit; recipients must actively search for employment. (329)*
9. What do the acronyms SNAP and EBT stand for. Where do recipients use EBT cards? *Supplemental Nutrition Assistance Program (SNAP) and Electronic Benefit Transfer (EBT). Recipients use EBT cards at participating grocery stores. (329)*
10. What role do you believe government should play in helping the poor? *Answers will vary.*

Lesson 53

1. What happened at Love Canal? *A chemical company dumped toxic waste there. Developers later built housing on the land and the city of Niagara Falls bought land for a school. People living there had health problems. The federal government undertook a major cleanup and relocated residents. (331)*
2. The Federal Register contains hundreds of thousands of pages of standards, guidelines, and rules that have the power of law in areas such as what? *Worker safety, product labeling, food handling, drug warnings, and advertising (332)*
3. Regulations are a limitation on what? *The free market (332)*
4. What is the purpose of regulations? *The public welfare (332)*

5. Why do regulations generally affect prices? *Producers pass the cost of complying with them on to consumers.* (332)
6. What was the result of the deregulation of the trucking industry? *Competition increased and transportation costs fell dramatically. (333)*
7. What was the result of the deregulation of the airline industry? *The reforms led to lower fares by increasing the ability of airlines to compete in a freer market. (333)*
8. What was the purpose of the Americans with Disabilities Act? *More equal physical access for all (333)*
9. What is the meaning of *caveat emptor*? *Let the buyer beware. (335)*
10. Do you believe that government regulation is more effective than self-regulation in a free market in which producers and consumers police themselves? Explain your answer. *Answers will vary.*

Lesson 54

1. Oliver Wendell Holmes Jr. said taxes are the price we pay for what? *Civilization (337)*
2. Give examples of itemized deductions. *Charitable contributions, medical expenses that exceed a certain percentage of taxable income, property and sales taxes paid, interest paid on a home mortgage (338)*
3. What does the term progressive tax mean? *The percentage of taxes to be paid increases as income rises. (339)*
4. What does the term regressive tax mean? *A higher percentage of income is paid in taxes at lower income levels. (339)*
5. How does a taxpayer determine his gross income? *By adding up all taxable income from wages, salaries, self-employment income, taxable investment income, and so forth (338)*
6. How does a taxpayer determine his taxable income? *By subtracting all exemptions and deductions from his or her gross income (338)*
7. How are payroll taxes different from an actual contribution to an account from which a person could draw from later? *They do not go into separate funds earmarked for Social Security and Medicare, but into the federal government's general revenue to pay for current expenses; some employees and self-employed persons will never receive the payments or services these taxes are supposed to fund. (340)*
8. Do you believe that it is better to tax income, consumption, or savings? Explain your answer. *Answers will vary.*
9. Do you believe that a flat tax is fair? Explain your answer. *Answers will vary.*
10. What is a Pigovian tax? *A tax that attempts to correct for negative externalities in market activity. (341)*

Lesson 55

1. What date marks the beginning of the federal government's fiscal year? *October 1 (344)*
2. What is discretionary spending? *Funding for programs that Congress is willing to reconsider (345)*
3. What is the multiplier effect? *Increased spending by the government which increases aggregate demand as those who receive federal dollars then use those dollars to buy goods and services (345)*
4. What is a deficit? *A deficit is the amount that the government spends each year which exceeds revenue that it receives. (345)*
5. What is the accumulated annual deficits of the United States called? *The national debt (345)*
6. When does the crowding out effect occur? *When deficit spending takes loanable funds from the money supply that could be used by businesses and allocates them to government programs (346)*
7. How is the federal deficit a moral issue? *To finance current expenses by imposing a legacy of debt on future generations is morally irresponsible (347)*
8. In philosophical terms, deficits are the government's attempt to defy what economics principle? *The principle of scarcity (346)*
9. What politically unpopular remedies for eradicating the national debt does the lesson mention? *Spending cuts, tax increases, or some combination of both (346)*
10. Copy the verse at the end of the lesson.
    The rich rules over the poor,
    And the borrower becomes the lender's slave.
    Proverbs 22:7 (348)

Unit 11 Quiz

6 points each

1. *government (319)*
2. *advisors (322)*
3. *trade representative (320)*
4. *management (322)*
5. *revenue (322)*
6. *subsidies (326)*
7. *fines (326)*
8. *defense (327)*
9. *increased (333)*
10. *itemized (338)*
11. *progressive (339)*
12. *discretionary (345)*
13. *deficit (345)*
14. *debt (345)*
15. *price (332)*

Opinion Question (10 points): Answers will vary.

Questions on *The Travels of a T-Shirt in the Global Economy*

1. From what perspective does the author write? What is her place in history, in geography, her background, her point of view and experience? How does her perspective influence the way she assesses and responds to her topic? Write one paragraph which includes your answers to all of these questions. *Answers will vary, but may include: Pietra Rivoli is a white American woman. Her life has spanned the late 20th and early 21st century. She is a professor in the Georgetown University business school in Washington, D.C. She has been trained in academic research. She is most likely accustomed to the American lifestyle, which is more prosperous than most of the rest of the world and the rest of history. Finding profitable work, providing for her basic needs, and buying a T-shirt are comparatively easy for someone like her. She obviously has compassion for the suffering of people and respect for hard work, innovation, and integrity. She traveled a great deal and spoke face-to-face with many people involved in the textile industry. She brings an open mind and is able to draw compassionate but honest conclusions.*
2. What do you feel are the key passages in the book? Think about the main conclusions and what supports them. What do these passages convey? What difference should these conclusions make in the thoughts and actions of the reader? Write three paragraphs. *Answers will vary,*
3. What other industry needs a treatment like The Travels of a T-shirt in the Global Economy? Why do you think so? What would you like to know about the truth of the industry? How do you think society would benefit? Write two or three paragraphs. *Answers will vary,*

Unit 12

Lesson 56

1. The gross domestic product is the market value of a nation's total domestic output of all final goods and services over a period of time. The gross domestic product consists of what components? *Purchases by consumers, purchases of capital goods by businesses, purchases of goods and services by government, and net exports (total exports minus total imports) (351)*
2. What is the gross national product? *The production of a nation's permanent residents, whether that production occurs within the country or elsewhere (351)*
3. What is considered a healthy annual rate of growth in the GDP? *3% (352)*
4. What is the nominal GDP? *The actual total figure of the value of the nation's output in terms of current prices (353)*
5. What does the real GDP express? *Output in terms of a comparison with the prices of goods and services in the previous year. (353)*
6. What is the statistic produced when the nominal GDP and the real GDP are compared? *GDP deflator (353)*
7. What does seasonal adjustment take into account? *Changes in economic activity that occur routinely throughout the year (353)*
8. What five countries have the largest economies? *United States, China, Japan, Germany, United Kingdom (352-353)*
9. How do economists calculate per capita GDP? *By dividing a country's GDP by its population (353)*
10. What does purchasing power parity (PPP) take into account? *The differences in the cost of living in various countries by using the long-term exchange rate between currencies to arrive at a common currency of expression (354)*

Lesson 57

1. What are the three most important macroeconomic variables? *The gross domestic product, the rate of inflation, and the rate of unemployment (356)*
2. What is the Consumer Price Index (CPI)? *An estimate of what a typical urban consumer has to pay for a sampling of typical goods and services (356)*
3. What is the basis for the CPI called? *A market basket of goods and services (357)*
4. What method does the Bureau of Labor Statistics use to measure unemployment? *A monthly survey of 60,000 homes (357)*
5. When was the Conference Board founded and what does it publish? *Leading Economic Index, or Index of Leading Economic Indicators (358)*
6. Why is unemployment a lagging indicator? *Because layoffs generally occur after sales have started to decline (358)*
7. What is disposable personal income (DPI)? *The money that households have available for discretionary spending after taxes (359)*
8. What does the Producer Price Index (PPI) reflect? Wholesale prices that producers charge to retail *establishments (359)*
9. What organization reports each month on the sale of new and existing homes and how the rate of sales compares with one year earlier? *The National Association of Realtors (359)*

10. What does the Bureau of Labor Statistics' quarterly reading of worker productivity reveal? *The average output per labor-hour (359)*

Lesson 58

1. What do people purchase in a stock market? *Shares of stock (that is, shares of ownership) in publicly traded corporations (361)*
2. What determines the prices of shares of stock? *The supply and demand of those stocks in the market (361)*
3. What is the largest actual stock market in the world and when did it begin? *The New York Stock Exchange (NYSE) began in 1792. (361)*
4. What company owns the New York Stock Exchange, where is its base, and what else does it own? *Intercontinental Exchange, based in Atlanta, owns the NYSE and other exchanges in Canada, Europe, and Singapore. (361)*
5. What does the Dow Jones Industrial Average do to create it's composite index? *It takes the stock values of thirty key companies out of the thousands traded on the NYSE and uses a formula to determine a cumulative value for those stocks. (362)*
6. What is the origin of the S&P 500? *In 1860, H. V. Poor published his first reference book with information on railroad companies. In 1906, the Standard Statistics Bureau company was organized to publish information about businesses other than railroads. (363)*
7. What is NASDAQ, where is it headquartered, when was it founded, and what type of stock market is it? *The National Association of Securities Dealers Automated Quotations, headquartered in New York City is an electronic stock market founded in 1971. (364)*
8. How do futures investors try to make money? *By taking risks on what stock and commodity prices will be in the future (365)*
9. What major commodities market is located in Chicago? *The Chicago Mercantile Exchange (364)*
10. The Dow Jones Industrial Average, the NASDAQ index, and the S&P 500 are fairly good indicators of what? What important portions of the economy are left out of those indices? *They indicate the perceived success of large companies that employ millions of people and that have a major impact on the economy. They do not take into account small businesses or the self-employed. (365-366)*

Lesson 59

1. What is the traditional definition of a recession? *When the gross domestic product has declined for at least two consecutive quarters or six months (367)*
2. Why do many economists not like that definition? *It does not consider any other variables such as unemployment or consumer confidence; they like to identify a more precise starting point for a recession. (367)*
3. List major measures of economic activity which decline or show only small growth during an economic downturn. *Stock prices, employment, personal income, business profits (367)*
4. What is the NBER? *The National Bureau of Economic Research (NBER) is a private, non-partisan, and non-profit organization founded in 1920 that conducts research on the economy. (368)*
5. When did it publish its first business cycle dates? *1929 (368)*
6. What is the official definition of a recession by the NBER? *"A significant decline in economic activity spread across the economy, lasting more than a few months, normally visible in real GDP, real income, employment, industrial production, and wholesale-retail sales." (368)*
7. What is the average length of a recession since World War II? *Eleven months (368)*
8. What has been the trend since World War II regarding the length of time between economic troughs? *They have gotten longer. (368)*
9. What did the Business Cycle Dating Committee of NBER determine were the two main factors in the recession that began in December 2007? *Domestic production and employment (368)*
10. What is the generally understood definition of a depression? *A period of economic downturn that is more severe than a recession. One common rule of thumb is that a depression involves a decline in the GDP of more than 10%. (369)*

Lesson 60

1. As of 2014, what was the median household income in the United States? *$53,657 (371)*
2. Approximately what percentage of American households have an income of $100,000 or more? What percentage of American households have an income under $20,000? *20%; 20% (371)*
3. What was Mollie Orshansky's standard for defining poverty? *Three times the amount of income needed for an economical food budget, adjusted for the number of persons in a household (371)*
4. How has the percentage of Americans living in poverty changed since the federal government began the War on Poverty in 1964? *It is not significantly different. (372)*
5. Define income. *Income is what a person earns during a certain period, usually one year. (373)*

6. Define wealth. *Wealth is the total value of a person's assets, which often includes a house and property, investments, bank accounts, and other useful goods, acquired over several years.* (373)
7. How do the poor in America compare to the poor in other countries? *Most of those who live in the lowest income quintile in the U.S. live in conditions that are vastly superior to the conditions in which most impoverished people in the world live. (373)*
8. Describe the typical home of a poor person, according to a 2005 survey. *It has three bedrooms, one and a half bathrooms, a garage, a porch or patio, and is in good repair. (373)*
9. What is the key issue for determining wealth and poverty? *Productivity (374)*
10. Are the poor poor because the rich are rich? Explain your answer. *Answers will vary.*

Unit 12 Quiz

1. *20% (371)*
2. *3% (352)*
3. *20% (371)*
4. *10% (369)*
5. *e (351)*
6. *j (351)*
7. *n (354)*
8. *a (356)*
9. *h (356)*
10. *c (358)*
11. *b (359)*
12. *p (361)*
13. *o (361)*
14. *f (362)*
15. *d (364)*
16. *g (364)*
17. *i (367)*
18. *k (368)*
19. *l (372)*
20. *m (373)*

Unit 13

Lesson 61

1. What fraction of the U.S. gross domestic product is devoted to health care? *One-sixth (381)*
2. What fraction of the federal budget goes to health care? *One-fourth (381)*
3. What is the purpose of insurance? *To share the risk of expense (382)*
4. The growth of health insurance caused what two effects? *Demand for medical treatment increased; increased demand drove up prices. (382)*
5. What is the meaning of moral hazard? *The tendency of people to engage in riskier behavior if other people bear or share the cost of that behavior. (383)*
6. What government program provides medical coverage for the elderly? The poor? *Medicare for the elderly; Medicaid for the poor (383)*
7. What is the comparison between the rise in medical costs and the rise of the overall rate of inflation? *Medical costs rise faster than inflation. (383)*
8. What does the Affordable Care Act of 2010 health care mandate? *Every American (with few exceptions) must have health insurance coverage or face the disincentive of having to pay a penalty. (384)*
9. Government involvement causes health care to be what kind of market? *Distorted (386)*
10. Do you believe that the federal government should be involved in health care? Explain your answer. *Answers will vary.*

Lesson 62

1. What was the original purpose of Social Security? *To provide retirement benefits for workers and survivor benefits to families of deceased workers (388)*
2. On what basis does the Social Security Administration calculate retirement benefits? *A worker's income during his years of work (388)*
3. Name two other terms used for Social Security taxes. *FICA which stands for Federal Insurance Contributions Act and payroll taxes (388)*
4. What type of benefits did Social Security begin paying in 1957? *Disability payments (388)*
5. What was the amount of Treasury bonds in the Social Security Trust Fund at the end of 2015? *$2.8 trillion (389)*
6. What are three reasons why Social Security is facing disaster? *More retirees are now living longer. The pool of workers paying into Social Security is shrinking. The first members of the Baby Boomer generation have become eligible for retirement. (389)*
7. Of the five potential solutions for Social Security mentioned in the lesson, which one do you think Congress should choose for America and why? *The answers to the why question will vary, but the five possible potential solutions are: Raise the full retirement age; use a means test to determine what level of benefits a person actually needs; lower the amount of benefits to individuals; increase the payroll tax rate; or raise the income ceiling above $118,500 or eliminate it. (391-392)*
8. What was the original purpose of Medicare? *To provide coverage for hospitalization and physician visits for Americans age 65 and older (391)*
9. What benefit did Congress add in 2003? *A prescription drug benefit (391)*
10. List five sources of revenue for Medicare. *Payroll taxes paid by working Americans; premiums paid by participants; general federal tax revenues; payments from states; interest earned by a trust fund devoted to the program (391)*

Lesson 63

1. What did coal make possible in the 1700s and 1800s? *The Industrial Revolution (394)*
2. When and where was the first petroleum well drilled in the United States? *Titusville, Pennsylvania in 1859 (395)*
3. What is OPEC? *The Organization of Petroleum Exporting Countries (395)*
4. What countries are members of OPEC? *Algeria, Angola, Ecuador, Iran, Iraq, Kuwait, Libya, Nigeria, Qatar, Saudi Arabia, United Arab Emirates, and Venezuela (395)*
5. What four main factors determined the price of gasoline in 2015? *The cost of crude oil; refining; federal and state taxes; and distribution, marketing, and dealer costs and profits (396)*
6. What country is the world's leading consumer of petroleum products? *The United States (396)*
7. What is the Strategic Petroleum Reserve? *An emergency supply of oil that the United States government has maintained in underground storage facilities along the Gulf of Mexico since 1975 (396)*
8. What are the two main problems associated with the use of fossil fuels for energy? *The supply that oil companies can recover is expected eventually to run out, and burning fossil fuels to produce energy generates atmospheric pollution. (394,397)*
9. What are two tradeoffs involved with the use of nuclear power? *The possibility of an accident that could release harmful radiation and the problem of what to do with radioactive waste that nuclear plants generate. (397)*
10. What has changed the market dynamics of alternative energy sources, such as wind and solar? *Developers have depended on large government subsidies. (398)*

Lesson 64

1. What was the key to Henry Ford's success with the Model T? *Making the car available to the mass market at a price that many people could afford (400)*
2. How much of the new car market did General Motors control in the 1950s? *Over half (400)*
3. What reduced the popularity of large American cars in the 1970s? *The price of gasoline (400)*
4. Why did the price of gasoline rise? *Oil-producing countries in the Middle East stopped selling oil to the United States because of this country's support of Israel. (400)*
5. What vehicle did Chrysler introduce in 1983 that revolutionized American car buying? *The minivan (401)*
6. Cars from what country began competing with American car manufacturing companies in the 1970s and 1980s? *Japan (401)*
7. What companies are the Big Three U.S. automakers? *General Motors, Ford, and Chrysler (401)*
8. List five businesses besides auto manufacturing that are dependent on vehicles. *Student should list five of these: new car dealers, used car dealers, repair shops, auto insurance companies, parts stores, gas stations, car washes, drive-in restaurants. (402)*
9. Name two ways that government regulations influence the automotive industry. *Exhaust emission standards and fuel efficiency regulations (403)*
10. Name the state that once had the most auto-related jobs and the state that now has the most auto-related jobs. *Michigan; Tennessee (404)*

Lesson 65

1. Why can houses, made of exactly the same building materials and with the same floor plan have widely varying values? *Location (406)*
2. What is a loan to purchase a home called? *Mortgage (406)*
3. Historically what has been the most common type of mortgage? *A loan for thirty years at a fixed rate of interest (406)*
4. What is an amortization table? *A chart showing the relative amounts of principal and interest in each payment over the life of the loan (406)*
5. Why is borrowing money to buy a home often considered to be a better idea than borrowing money to buy a car? *Because a home is expected to increase in value while a car will almost certainly decrease in value over time (407)*
6. How does the Federal Housing Authority encourage and assist home ownership? *By insuring some mortgages that private banks make to homeowners (408)*
7. What two government-sponsored investment corporations buy mortgages that lending institutions issue and what are their nicknames? *Federal National Mortgage Association (nicknamed Fannie Mae) and the Federal Home Loan Mortgage Corporation (nicknamed Freddie Mac) (408)*
8. What government-owned corporation guarantees bonds that are backed by home mortgages that are insured by a government agency, usually the FHA or the VA and what is its nickname? *The Government National Mortgage Association (Ginnie Mae) (409)*

9. What three tax incentives does the federal government give to people who buy a home? *The ability to deduct home mortgage interest; the ability to deduct property taxes from taxable income; and when a person sells a house, not having to pay capital gains taxes on the first $250,000 that the house has gained in value (409)*
10. When can home mortgages have a negative impact on the economy? *When a family has such a large mortgage, it must cut back on other purchases and when a homeowner defaults on a mortgage and the lending agency has to sell the home for less than it is worth (409)*

Unit 13 Quiz

1. *moral hazard (383)*
2. *Medicare (383)*
3. *Medicaid (383)*
4. *Affordable Care Act of 2010 (384)*
5. *Social Security (388)*
6. *disability payments (388)*
7. *Baby Boomer generation (389)*
8. *hospitalization, physician visits (391)*
9. *Industrial Revolution (394)*
10. *petroleum, Qatar (395)*
11. *Strategic (396)*
12. *subsidies (398)*
13. *minivan (401)*
14. *Japan (401)*
15. *General Motors, Chrysler (401)*
16. *Michigan, Tennessee (404)*
17. *mortgage (406)*
18. *interest (406)*
19. *Fannie Mae (408)*
20. *capital gains (409)*

Unit 14

Lesson 66

1. How many farms did America have in 1860? *About two million (413)*
2. How did states finance land grant universities? *Selling public lands (414)*
3. How did land grant universities aid farming? *Teaching college courses in improved farming methods and conducting scientific research to aid farming (414)*
4. Give two examples of groups which worked to aid farmers in the late 1800s. *The Grange and the Populist Party (414)*
5. What were the primary means by which the federal government became involved in farming during the New Deal? *Price supports and crop restrictions (414)*
6. How many farms did America have in the 1940s and in 2014? *About six million; just over two million (414)*
7. List ten technological and scientific advancements that helped to increase farm yield. *Steel-tipped plow, the reaper, the combine, railroads, motorized farm equipment, seeds, fertilizer, pesticides, computers, satellite technology (414)*
8. What is America's largest crop? What fuel do American companies produce from it? *Corn, ethanol (416)*
9. What is the Renewable Fuel Mandate? *A requirement by Congress that oil refiners include ethanol in an increasing percentage of the gasoline they produce (416)*
10. How is organic farming different from conventional farming? *Organic farmers use non-chemical means to produce foods. (416)*

Lesson 67

1. What environmental catastrophe happened in Flint, Michigan, in 2014? *The city began utilizing the Flint River for city water, but officials had not properly treated the water for contaminants. (419)*
2. What federal agency was founded in 1970? *The Environmental Protection Agency (419)*
3. What two groups have been the main adversaries in the debate over environmental policy? *Environmentalists and conservationists, and business interests (419)*
4. What 1962 book by Rachel Carson pointed to the serious negative environmental consequences of widespread use of DDT? Silent Spring *(419)*
5. Describe the tradeoffs involved in mining gold and copper at the open-pit Pebble Mine in southwest Alaska. *The mine would ruin a salmon habitat, release toxic mine waste into the environment, damage a beautiful location, and cause the loss of thousands of jobs in the salmon fishing industry. (420)*
6. What is cost-benefit analysis about? *Deciding if the cost of doing something is worth making the choice (420)*
7. What do economic activity and growth require and what is the result of economic activity and growth? *They require energy; they result in waste. (420)*

8. What are three negative consequences to the government formulating regulations? *A bureaucracy must enforce them, they result in endless legal battles, and they usually wind up costing everybody money that could be put to better use. (421)*
9. How does cap and trade work in theory? *Government grants allotments to industries of how much carbon emissions the industries can produce (the cap), and then issues permits that companies buy at auction which allow the companies to produce carbon emissions above their initial allotments (the trade). (422)*
10. What is your personal opinion about climate change? *Answers will vary.*

Lesson 68

1. What two formulas are used to express productivity? *Output/inputs and output/hours worked (425)*
2. What formula expresses productivity for an economy as a whole? *GDP/aggregate hours worked (425)*
3. List three factors involved in inputs. *Time, number of people employed, resources used (425)*
4. How did technology affect the productivity of Betty the seamstress? *The sewing machine made her more productive than Carol, who sewed by hand. (426)*
5. Who helped staff the growing number of factories, especially in the late 1800s and early 1900s? *Immigrants (427)*
6. If you were starting a landscaping business or a babysitting service, do you think you would be more like Tom or Hank? *Answers will vary.*
7. What limitations does the lesson mention as examples of why a country might have low productivity? *Insufficient materials, unreliable electrical service, poorly-maintained machines. (427)*
8. How can a national government encourage investment? *By keeping tax, debt, and inflation rates low and by maintaining stable financial markets (428)*
9. How does economic growth lessen poverty? *By creating new opportunities for employment and for entrepreneurs to make profits (428)*
10. Copy Proverbs 10:4. *Poor is he who works with a negligent hand, but the hand of the diligent makes rich. Proverbs 10:4 (429)*

Lesson 69

1. What was the process of buying stocks on margin in the 1920s? *People only put down 10-25 percent of the stock values and borrowed the rest from the broker. (430)*
2. On what day did the stock market lose 13% of its value? *October 29, 1929 (431)*
3. In the 1930s, why did banks not have enough money to satisfy depositors' demands? *Because they operated on a fractional reserve basis, they did not have money to give to depositors who began wanting their money in cash. (431)*
4. What was the result of the Smoot-Hawley Tariff Congress passed in 1930? *A sharp drop in trade with other countries (431)*
5. Why had Congress lowered income tax rates during the 1920s? *Because the federal government had begun running a surplus (432)*
6. Why did the Roosevelt Administration try to decrease production? *Because they believed that too much competition had led to overproduction (433)*
7. How did the length of the Great Depression in the United States compare with its length in many other countries? *It was several years longer in the U.S. than it was in many other countries. (433)*
8. What is the top marginal income tax rate? *The rate paid by people with the highest income (433)*
9. Why did raising taxes to 90% by 1944 hurt the possibility of investment? *Those with the highest incomes had less money to invest (434)*
10. When did production and employment increase significantly? *When military production increased dramatically during World War II (433)*

Lesson 70

1. What were three factors that contributed to the 2008 recession? *Debt, government encouragement of homeownership, and greed (435)*
2. What was the economic boom of the late 1990s called? *The high-tech bubble (436)*
3. What is a subprime mortgage? *A mortgage given to a borrower who is not a prime candidate for a mortgage (436)*
4. What terms refer to investment instruments containing a bundle of mortgage loans? *Mortgage-backed securities (436)*
5. What is a derivative? *A financial instrument whose value is determined by or derived from an underlying asset (436)*
6. What is the term for a bank taking over a home that has a mortgage? *A foreclosure (436)*
7. What is commercial paper? *Short term loans companies obtain to make their payroll (437)*
8. What did taxpayers receive as a result of the Economic Stimulus Act Congress passed in February 2008? *Checks totaling about $152 billion (437)*

9. What did the federal government do for Bear Stearns in 2008 and GM in 2009? *It assumed $30 billion in liabilities from Bear Stearns and took controlling interest in GM. (437)*
10. What is a credit default swap? *A kind of insurance arrangement in which a bank or investment company that holds a debt makes a payment like a premium to an insurance company, for which the insurance company assumes the risk if the debt goes bad (437-438)*

Unit 14 Quiz

1. *land grant (414)*
2. *satellite (415)*
3. *corn (416)*
4. *ethanol (416)*
5. *mandate (416)*
6. *organic (416)*
7. *Flint (419)*
8. *protection (419)*
9. *business (419)*
10. *cost-benefit (420)*
11. *inputs (422)*
12. *productivity (427)*
13. *investment (428)*
14. *poverty (428)*
15. *margin (430)*
16. *fractional (431)*
17. *marginal (433)*
18. *spend (432)*
19. *greed (435)*
20. *bubble (436)*
21. *subprime (436)*
22. *securities (436)*
23. *commercial (437)*
24. *General Motors (438)*
25. *stock market (431)*

Unit 15

Lesson 71

1. How do individuals make a difference in the economy? *Individuals make economic decisions, develop products and services, consider opportunity costs, face tradeoffs, and deal with unintended consequences. (443)*
2. In what tension between two realities do Christians live? *The spiritual realm and the physical world (443-444)*
3. What are some economic responsibilities that Christians have? *To have hearts of compassion for the poor and for victims of injustice, to provide for themselves, and to teach others to do the same (444)*
4. Give an example of an area of your life where you depend on God while also working. *Answers will vary.*
5. Tell why you had rather be a contributor instead of being dependent on the government. *Answers will vary.*
6. In what way(s) would you like to be a contributor to the economy and to the betterment of society? *Answers will vary.*
7. In what ways are you called on to do the right thing regardless of what others do? *Specific circumstances will vary.*
8. Name one activity that you are involved in that reveals your commitment to God. *Answers will vary.*
9. Name a business practice that you have witnessed that you believe revealed a lack of integrity and tell how you would handle that situation differently. *Answers will vary.*
10. Do you plan to vote when you reach the legal voting age? Why? Why not? *Answers will vary.*

Lesson 72

1. Define moral economy. *Economic activity based on moral principles such as goodness, fairness, honesty, and justice (447)*
2. What is necessary for markets to bring about mutually satisfying exchanges? *Trust (447)*
3. When was the moral economy easier to maintain? *When market activity was concentrated in local communities (447)*
4. What is one practical way that you keep the long term in mind? *Answers will vary.*
5. How does paying bills on time show respect for others? *Answers will vary.*
6. How could someone who works in government bless others in his work? *Answers will vary.*
7. Name three needs that you would like to help through charitable giving. *Answers will vary.*
8. In what ways have your parents worked to train your conscience? *Answers will vary.*
9. Why might elderly people benefit from having a small local grocery store available? *Answers will vary.*
10. What does your own conscience tell you about socially responsible or conscience funds? *Answers will vary.*

Lesson 73

1. What is Charlie Shedd's financial plan? *Give ten percent, save ten percent, and live on the rest with thanksgiving and praise. (451)*
2. List five of your own financial goals. *Answers will vary.*
3. What are the two most important elements of a budget? *Making it and keeping it (452)*
4. List six components of housing expenses. *Rent or mortgage payment, utilities, insurance, maintenance, furnishings, and improvements (452)*
5. What does it mean to live within your means? *If you can't afford a purchase within your budget, save up for it or generate more income. (453)*

6. Define what it means for a borrower to be the slave of a lender. *Answers will vary.*
7. What does insurance manage? *Risk (453)*
8. What do many Christians purchase as an alternative to health insurance? *A health expense sharing plan (453)*
9. What is bankruptcy? *The inability to pay one's debts (453)*
10. What is the standard of living that Jesus offers? *Eternal life (454)*

Lesson 74

1. What is a leader? *Someone who influences others (457)*
2. List three leaders whom you respect. *Answers will vary.*
3. In what sense is impacting the economy from the home returning economics to its roots? *The English word economics used to mean the management of a home. (457)*

4-10. Taking off from the quotation by Frederich Buechner above, what is your deep gladness? What great need in the world do you believe you can fill? Answer with a paragraph. *Answers will vary.*

Lesson 75

1. Where do we go for a field trip for this lesson? *To the Sermon on the Mount or on a mountain in Israel (459)*
2. What kind of righteousness does Jesus call for? *A righteousness of the heart and not just outward actions (459)*
3. What does Jesus say about the practice of religion? *Not to make a show of it (459)*
4. What does Jesus want us to store up? *Heavenly riches (460)*
5. What does your treasure show? *Where your heart is (460)*
6. What is the way to spiritual wealth? *Putting God first (460)*
7. What two illustrations in the created world does Jesus use? *Birds, flowers (460-461)*
8. What should be your first priority? *To make sure that God is your king and that His way of righteousness is your way of living (461)*
9. How does Jesus expect us to respond to His words? *He expects us to act upon His words, to put them into practice, to do them. (462)*
10. How can Christians most effectively participate in the economy? *When they see themselves as oikonomoi, stewards of the resources that God places in their care (462)*

Unit 15 Quiz

1. *a, i, n, s, y (443)*
2. *c, p (444)*
3. *v (447)*
4. *e (447)*
5. *b, k, t (451)*
6. *w, g (452)*
7. *d, f, h, j, o, x (452)*
8. *q (453)*
9. *l (453)*
10. *u (462)*
11. *m, z (459)*
12. *r (454)*

Questions on *Mover of Men and Mountains*

1. In two or three paragraphs, write a synopsis and review of Mover of Men and Mountains. *Answers will vary.*
2. What do you think was LeTourneau's purpose in writing his autobiography? Write one paragraph answering this question. *Answers will vary.*
3. Write two or three paragraphs about a person you know who is a servant of the Lord in a "secular" job. How does this person honor God through his or her work? What special opportunities does his or her career provide for ministry? *Answers will vary.*

Third Exam answers on next page.

Third Exam (Units 11-15)

(3 points each):

1. *Council of Economic Advisors (322)*
2. *United States Trade Representative (322)*
3. *Office of Management and Budget (322)*
4. *Internal Revenue Service (322)*
5. *New York Stock Exchange (361)*
6. *NASDAQ (364)*
7. *Chicago Mercantile Exchange (364)*
8. *Fannie Mae (408)*
9. *Medicare (328)*
10. *Medicaid (328)*
11. *Social Security (388)*
12. *War on Poverty (372)*

True/False (2 points each):

13. *True (322, 398)*
14. *True (338)*
15. *False (the term is deficit) (345)*
16. *False (Chrysler introduced the minivan) (401)*
17. *True (351)*
18. *True (351)*
19. *False (typical urban consumer) (356)*
20. *True (361)*
21. *False (moral hazard) (383)*
22. *False (2010) (384)*
23. *False (eleven months) (368)*
24. *False (Organization of Petroleum Exporting Countries) (395)*
25. *False (mortgage) (406)*
26. *True (409)*
27. *False (corn) (416)*
28. *True (425)*
29. *False (less money) (337)*
30. *True (436-437)*
31. *True (447)*
32. *True (454)*
33. *True (453)*
34. *False (the spiritual and the physical) (444)*
35. *True (452)*
36. *True (453)*
37. *False (high-tech) (436)*

Summarize five main things you have learned from *Exploring Economics* (14 points total). *Answers will vary.*